P9-DIZ-085

More TEA LEAVES

Devotional Meditations for Women

Written by twelve mothers, missionaries at home and abroad.
(See biographical sketches on pages 367–373.)

Compiled by
Nancy Stutzman

The Best in Wholesome Reading
Choice Books of Northern Virginia
P.O. Box 4080
Manassas, VA 20108-4080
We Welcome Your Response

Christian Light Publications, Inc.
Harrisonburg, VA 22802

MORE TEA LEAVES

Christian Light Publications, Inc.,
Harrisonburg, Virginia 22802
© 2000 by Christian Light Publications, Inc.
All rights reserved. Published 2000
Printed in the United States of America

09 08 07 06 05 04 03 02 01 00   5 4 3 2 1

An attempt has been made to secure permission for the use of all copyrighted material. If further information is received, the publisher will be glad to properly credit such material in future printings.

Cover photo: Judy Martin
Cover design: David W. Miller
Artists: Anne Miller, Ruth Yoder, Margaret Beachy,
          and Dale Hochstedler

ISBN: 0-87813-592-8

**Dedicated
To our godly mothers:**

Christina

Fannie

Katie

Lutisha

Mae

Mary

Mary

Mary

Susan

Suvilla

Wilma

When *Tea Leaves* was published in 1990, we couldn't have imagined the results. Ten years and over 115,000 copies later, the testimonies of a dozen missionary and ministers' wives are still reaching the hearts of women. *Tea Leaves* has been read and reread, shared with friends, and given as gifts.

Now, we are happy to bring you *More Tea Leaves*, with fresh, new devotional meditations by women for women. Most of the original writers are back, with the addition of two new writers. All have seen years in Christian service, learning and practicing what they write.

We appreciate the willingness of the writers and compiler to share from their hearts. May God use these quiet, Scriptural meditations to minister to the heart of every woman who reads the pages of *More Tea Leaves*.

The Publishers

Acknowledgements

I am grateful to:

❖ God. He gave us time and thoughts. He guided as we wrote. He protected as entries were delivered by postal systems, boat, and bus, or in Tim's backpack. Much more, He protected this manuscript, packed away in a puny plastic bucket when Hurricane Mitch threatened to wash away all earthly possessions.

❖ David, my companion and most faithful encourager. You caught the vision and, with patient persistence, cheered me on.

❖ My daughters: Lou Ann, Marsha, and Melissa. You stood by me and lifted up my hands by putting your own to many unexciting household tasks.

❖ Glen and Salome for the hours you spent critiquing my work. Your support and enthusiasm were invaluable.

❖ Julia and Denise, helpers in our home. How could I count the ways you assisted?

❖ My mother and many others who prayed.

Nancy Stutzman, Compiler

Preface

How was *More Tea Leaves* born? This time it was born through the vision of men, the publishers and our husbands, who were convinced that *Tea Leaves* met needs.

We writers considered hesitantly. We remembered the cost: time, effort, and vulnerability. Ten years later it's no easier. We are busy homeschooling, caring for toddlers and sick husbands, answering calls (radio, telephone, and door), and making a living. Writing takes tremendous effort when you are in continual physical or emotional pain. It would be easier to keep our failures and problems unexposed. But we also have comfort and hope to share, for God is so gracious.

Ten years made a difference in our locations. Only four of us are on foreign mission fields. One, Esther Herschberger, was called to her eternal Home in 1995. How we miss her.

These "leaves" are not perfect, just as the writers are not perfect. But, like the writers and you, each has its own unique spot. We share with you a strong desire to let the Master Editor work on us. While we fill our own special places on earth, He works: erasing sins, adding graces, rearranging people and circumstances in our lives. He purposes to present us faultless, entries into the Book of Eternity.

The Compiler

CONTENTS

2. Let . . . the Wife . . . Reverence Her Husband

3. He Maketh . . . (Her) to Be a Joyful Mother

4. Be At Peace Among Yourselves

5. After This Manner ... The Holy Women ... Adorned Themselves

6. Cleanse Thou Me From Secret Faults

7. Being Filled With the Fruits of Righteousness

8. My Grace Is Sufficient for Thee

9. Continue in Prayer . . .
With Thanksgiving

10. I Will Open My Mouth in a Parable

11. Holding Forth the Word of Life

CHAPTER ONE

"With My Whole Heart Have I Sought Thee"

Psalm 119:10

Time to Listen

Psalm 86

O God,
    I am grateful
That, though You are
So busy running Your vast
            universe,
    when I come to You in prayer.
Anytime,
        anywhere,
            with any need,
    You are ready to bow down
            Your ear
    to this, Your lowly handmaid.
    With shame I confess that
    too often I am only half listening
    when my daughter comes to me
    with an interesting happening
    or my husband needs help finding
    that misplaced receipt *now.*
    Your Perfect Example
            spurs me
    to greater faithfulness.
    Thank You for Your love
            and patience
            with me.

        With love,
            Your daughter

We See Jesus

Hebrews 2:9-18

I saw Jesus! No, not in person, but in a picture our new teacher put up at our Christian school. When I first saw the "modern art" of senseless blobs and dots entitled, "Christ," I was disappointed at the lack of reverence for the Saviour. We asked our teacher about it.

He replied enthusiastically. If you focus your eyes beyond the blobs and dots, you will see Jesus on the cross, and in the bottom corners, a nativity scene and an empty tomb. The quest began. Day after day his students (and their parents) stood in front of that picture in search of Christ. Today I tried again.

My eyes were glued to the picture. Suddenly, the blobs began shifting and forming shapes. Something was emerging from the intricate confusion of patterns. And there was Jesus! A three-dimensional picture.

I gazed at the blobs, wondering where He came from— and He was gone. I shifted my focus off the blobs (it takes effort), and there He was! The longer I gazed, the more details I saw. It was astonishing.

There's a lesson here. When my life seems to become a bunch of meaningless blobs, as happens sometimes, I want to concentrate and focus on the Crucified and Risen One. When I "see" Him, I realize life's "senseless" trials have a purpose for my good.

My Eyes Are On Thee

Psalm 119:73-80

A while ago I came home from church,
and entered the house.
My children were all around me,
But no husband—no David.
I missed that person who had loved me,
Who encouraged that little person in me.
I had just worshiped God.
I had taught the women's Sunday school class.
I felt God had touched the class with the lesson.
But I longed for David,
To share the richness of our spiritual lives.
I longed for that depth of interchange with him.
But he had slipped away from me
Nearly two years ago already.

I ached so much that I had to talk.
I went to my twin and her husband.
Tears flowed
As they felt my anguish and loss;
My desire and need.
When finally they spoke
They quoted a song—
    "Turn your eyes upon Jesus.
      Look full in His wonderful face,
        And the things of earth will grow strangely dim
          In the light of His glory and grace."[1]

[1]Chorus from "Turn Your Eyes Upon Jesus" by Helen H. Lemmel

Lord, I bow before You again.
Take this aching heart
That knew such love, such oneness
As we together worshiped You.
I raise my head—and heart.
My eyes are on You.
Fill this void with Your being.
I know Your ways are right.
I cannot count Your tender mercies toward me.
My eyes are on You.
Stability, solace, comfort, and strength
Are drawn from You and Your Word.
Above all else I need You—and
I await the joy of heaven.

Easter

Luke 24:1-7

*D*ear friends, I want to tell you
That Easter means to me
That Christ the king of Glory
Shall reign eternally.

That little tomb in Palestine
Could not my Saviour hold!
He burst the bars of sin and death
And left that prison cold.

So, praise the Lord, I now can live
And in my soul have peace,
For Jesus came into my heart
And gave me sweet release.

And when, oh, joy, that day He'll come
And take me home above,
I still shall talk about His grace
And sing of all His love.

Doors

John 10:1-11

*L*ord, I saw a sign in Belize City that read, "Through this door pass the most important people in the world." A Christmas card from a wholesaler echoed the thought, "Through this door pass the world's finest people, our customers."

I thought about doors—open doors and closed doors.

Open doors invite me inside either to satisfy my curiosity or to receive what I already know is waiting for me. I love to go to my parents' house. Being able to enter their open door only once every few years makes me especially thankful to You for the love and acceptance I find inside.

Closed doors signal rejection or unavailability. The baby was sick. I went to the doctor's private clinic. But the door was shut. He was not available to help me.

Lord, You said, "I am the door." I'm glad You are always an open door to me. When I first entered in by You, the Door, I was curious. What did you have to offer? Now I know, and enter because I find safety, security, and love in abundance.

I'm glad you are the Open Door to others. I can point anyone to You and know You will always accept them too.

When I think of You, Lord, I say "Through this Door pass the most loved people in all the world."

Jesus, the Bread and Water of Life

John 6:27-35

*W*e get hungry and thirsty. We hunger and thirst for fulfillment and happiness. People often focus on music, clothes, food, conveniences, relationships, vehicles, money, sports, trips, or hobbies in a frantic search for meaning.

Proverbs 27:7b aptly describes this emptiness in our lives when it says, "To the hungry soul every bitter thing is sweet." Isaiah's rebuke in the first verses of Chapter 55 could have been written today: "Wherefore do ye spend money for that which is not bread? and your labour for that which satisfieth not?"

We can even seek for happiness in doing all the right things, such as reading our Bibles, praying, or memorizing Scriptures. Spiritual exercise is good and right, but if our motives are wrong, we can't receive the blessings God would give us.

The most important thing in life is a relationship with Jesus Christ. This relationship is the only satisfying solution to our hunger and thirst. It is the lasting answer to our needs. Nothing whatsoever can replace it. Jesus is the only source of joy that is rich, deep, fulfilling, abiding, and true. We *cannot*, we *may not* look to anyone or anything else for that joy and happiness.

God Fills My Need

Psalm 42

*G*od, You know I grow weary.
There is so much to do,
  so many people who need me—
    my husband, my children,
      my friends, and the church.
At times I am burdened,
  and feel overwhelmed
    with the needs, the problems,
      the concerns of so many people
        pressing upon me.
To my husband, I am a help-mate,
  to my children, a care-giver;
    To my friends, an encourager,
      listening to their problems.

Sometimes I am a counselor and advisor.
But at times I cry out,
  "Who will be *my* friend, *my* counselor,
    who will mother *me?*"
Then, God, I remember
  that You created me.
    You understand my needs,
      better than anyone else ever could!
And I rest assured, comforted,
  at peace in Your love for me.

I Sent My Son

1 John 4:9-12

*W*hen Eli was kidnapped, his captors sent me this message: "Send your oldest son with $11,500. He must deliver the ransom alone. If we don't have the money by two o'clock tomorrow afternoon, we'll kill your husband."

How could I let Ernest go up that mountain to deliver the ransom? I needed him. He possessed a maturity I had never seen in him before.

For the first time, our roles were reversed. Now Ernest was strong; I was weak. He cared for me; I depended on him. I wept on his chest; he embraced and reassured me.

My love for my husband made me want to pay the ransom as quickly as possible. My love for my son made me want to hold him back. I felt torn between love for my husband and love for my son.

After an agony of indecision, I knew I must send Ernest to deliver the ransom. After weeping in his arms once more, I kissed him goodbye. He carried the big package of money to the pickup and drove away. With a breaking heart, I turned to the One who sent His only Son to deliver the ransom for me.

My heavenly Father, who didn't spare His own Son from that dangerous mission, now filled me with strength and peace while my son went on his. God allowed His own Son to die at the hands of His captors, but He gave mine back to me, along with my husband.

Now I have a deeper appreciation for the love that compelled God to send His Son to deliver the ransom for me. That love sustained me in one of the most difficult situations I have ever faced.

Acknowledgement

John 16:17-23

*L*ord Jesus,
    I am ashamed
    I don't understand
    Or fully appreciate
    What my birth cost You.

True, Lord,
    My children don't know
    The suffering experienced
    Through their birth.
    They cannot guess
    The joy I felt
    At their birth.

No, Lord,
    I don't expect them
    To comprehend.
    I simply want them to
    Trust me,
    Love me,
    Obey me, and
    Acknowledge me before others.

Dear Lord,
    Is that what You want
    From me?

Serving and Worship

Luke 10:38-42

I love the account of Mary and Martha in Luke, Chapter 10. I often find myself wanting to sit at Jesus' feet as did Mary, but needing to be busy with daily work and serving as was Martha. My family and other people require my time. There are meals to prepare, dishes to wash, and laundry awaiting my attention. I want to keep my house clean and comfortable. The work is endless.

Martha loved Jesus too. She showed her love to Jesus with a good meal. She was concerned about His physical needs. Jesus did not rebuke Martha for being a server. Jesus rebuked her for being cumbered. Another translation says, "worried and upset." Martha lost a blessing by becoming more concerned over the details of the physical preparations than the joy of serving Jesus!

We, too, need to find time to sit at Jesus' feet and worship as Mary did. At times the work will wait while we spend quiet time alone with God. We may need to wake up in the morning before the children or set aside a regular time of day to pray and read God's Word.

God desires our service *and* our worship!

A Daily Memorial

Joshua 3:14–4:8

I am fascinated when I read this passage of Joshua leading the Israelites across the Jordan River. Why did God choose to have them cross during the time of year when the river overflowed its banks? They saw the water swirling around the priests' ankles, only to stop flowing and begin backing up! It was a miracle to remember!

And God wanted them to remember it. He commanded that a memorial be made of stones from the river. Just as Joshua used stones for a memorial, we can experience a daily memorial, an encounter with the Lord. As we commune with God in the early morning, meditate on His Word, and pour out our hearts to Him, we establish a memorial to Him.

Many times when facing temptation or a struggle during the day, I have remembered the Scripture I read, or I have seen God answering a prayer I prayed that morning. Recalling the early morning encounter with God has, indeed, become a memorial to me.

How can we make this daily memorial experience more meaningful? Prepare a small devotional basket. In my basket I have my well-marked Bible. The next important item to me is my prayer journal. This is a blank notebook I have divided into four sections using the acronym, ACTS. These categories are: adoration, confession, thanksgiving, and supplication. I find that writing my prayers in these categories keeps me focused. My basket also contains other devotional books for inspirational reading, a pack of tissues, and a pen for marking passages. You may want to include other things in yours.

Are you building daily memorials to God? Whether facing temptation or experiencing joy in your life, it will help you remember.

In His Presence

Psalm 139:1-10

*O*ne morning I was feeling harried. Things weren't falling into place as I had hoped. I felt grumpy as my fifth-grade son and I sat on the well-worn living room couch to read the day's assignment in his Bible workbook. It was a new workbook. We opened it and read the three section titles. I noted the workbook's theme was "The Presence of God."

The 45 plus years' worth of sermons, topics, and seminars I've heard didn't keep my eleven-year-old's words from penetrating. "He is everywhere at once. He hears people pray at the same time all over the world. Whenever we need God's help, He is there protecting us."

As we continued, I was touched by the reality of God's presence. The phrase, "In Thy presence is fullness of joy," gripped me. Gulp! Fullness of joy? I was still feeling irked at how my morning had gone.

"Oh, Lord," I prayed, "please forgive me for being grumpy and unthankful. Cleanse my heart of all ungratefulness and help me realize more fully that Your presence gives joy. Thank You for being here and for the joy You give."

My workload didn't suddenly become lighter, but my footsteps did. The pressures I was facing didn't escape me, but a sense of His Presence had set me free. The simple words, "In Thy presence is fullness of joy," made the difference.

Apron Pockets and Sheltering Wings

Psalm 91

*J*ennifer received some sweets on the last day of school. She was, of course, delighted. When she went outside, she carefully placed her treasure on the table and asked me to keep it safely for her. Then, thinking better of her decision, she scooped up the handful of candy and dropped it into my apron pocket.

Upon her return, she came straight to my pocket and reclaimed her treat. We were both satisfied: Jennifer, because her treasure was still where she had left it, and I, because I had kept her trust.

Mama's apron pocket equaled safety and security.

My thoughts turn to God. Does *He* have apron pockets? Hardly. But the Psalm speaks of a secret place, feathers, and sheltering wings. Jesus promised that as His followers, we are in God's hands, and no one can take us out. Paul, too, was confident of God's keeping until the close of his earthly life.

What a refreshing view of God as Father! If it gave me pleasure to fulfill my daughter's request, how much more does it satisfy God's Father-heart to do the same for me? What more could I want? *His* keeping is constant and never-failing—better than a mother's care could ever be. What perfect security! How blessed I am to be His child!

The Truth

John 4:7-14

A woman, hungry for fresh veggies, is standing at the sales counter outside our porch. She buys and we chat. She is friendly, and since business is slow, the conversation goes on. One thing leads to another.

I ask if she knows what it means to be born again. Her answer tells me volumes. Though she grew up in a church, she is clueless about a genuine life in Christ. I briefly explain the change Jesus has made in my life.

I discover my friend believes in reincarnation, embraces Buddhism, and loves the Dalai Lama. She tries to do good to her fellowman, *but admits she's unsatisfied.*

We exchange addresses and she is gone. I feel sad. My new friend is only passing through, so I may never see her again. What events in her life led her to such a worldview? Such confusion! Such darkness!

As I gaze thoughtfully into the evening twilight, I feel a deep gratitude for the Truth, grateful to have been taught the Bible from my childhood, grateful that my parents didn't separate like hers did, grateful to know *personally* the One who created me and died for me.

How liberating the Truth is! How powerful it is! It brings light, the opposite of darkness. It brings gladness and joy, the opposite of emptiness and sadness. The Truth satisfies. I need not look for "something more." I have found the Living Water, which satisfies that dreadful thirst.

Delight of God

Jeremiah 17:7-10

*T*he Lord set me down again. In fact, laid me down flat on my back with the flu. I sense He wants my attention focused on Him.

I wanted to be busy: scrubbing floors, cooking for my family, sewing a pair of pajamas, cleaning a closet, or visiting a neighbor. I wanted to be about and doing things and enjoying life. I like to accomplish things, feel equal to a task, and keep up with my work. I chafe at being sick.

"Thy will be done on earth." Yes, Lord, in my small corner of the earth, what would You have me do today? Did You allow this sickness so that I would have time (and plenty of it) to meditate on You? Did You want me to evaluate my priorities and look at things from Your perspective?

What does God value? Does He delight in a multitude of things accomplished, or in hearts that are tuned to Him? Is He pleased with homey duties done as unto Him? Does a child of His, fervently sharing the Gospel, bring more honor to Him than another of His own who quietly accepts a time of illness? Does God compare His children with each other (as we humans tend to) by what we see on the surface? Are we precious to Him for what we accomplish?

Dear ones, God sees and knows our hearts.
He delights in hearts
that He has cleansed from sin,
hearts that now commune with Him.

Quiet hearts,
    at peace, at rest
        with what He chooses.
Hearts that throb to do His will,
    fulfill His calling,
        and seek His kingdom now.
Obedient hearts,
    content in humble walks and homey tasks
        if God is there.
Hearts who find
    their joy, their life, their all,
        in Him.

God Made This Day?

Psalm 118

his is the day which the LORD *hath made; we will rejoice and be glad in it"* (Psalm 118:24).

How easy it is to say this verse when the sun is shining, my day is going as planned, or a friend I've been longing to see stops in for tea. But what about cold and drizzly days when the children are underfoot; the hours get sliced into useless bits and pieces by the phone, the doorbell, and childish squabbles; and I am shaken by an uncomfortable confrontation. Is *this* a day God made?

My earliest memory of this verse is when I was seven years old. The Lord had called my 14-month-old brother home to be with Him. The morning of the funeral, I was in the kitchen when Daddy came in from the mailbox. In the mail was a calendar from the American Bible Society with this verse on it. I vividly remember how he put his arm around Mom and, with tears streaming down his cheeks, read, "This is the day *which* the LORD hath made; we will rejoice and be glad in it." I remember my parents showing that attitude throughout that time of grief.

When God allows trials to touch my life and take away what is dear and enjoyable to me, do I rebelliously ask, "Why?" I want to say with the psalmist, "This is the day which the LORD hath made," and rejoice.

Why Did I Question God?

2 Corinthians 9:6-11

*E*arly this spring the mission board asked if I would consider letting my son Kevin go to the Dominican Republic mission for the summer.

I wept. I wished David could help me decide. I wanted so much that David and I could seek God's answer for our son together. But I did not have David. I did have two sons who were bringing in most of the income for the family. And the mission board was gently asking if one of them could go to the DR. Would God ask that sacrifice of me too?

I spent three days in grief, missing David, needing David. And as I grieved for him, God gave me my answer.

In the years he was with us, David had stressed God's care for us. He would say, "If you are looking to me, I may fail. God is our Provider. If we trust God and His Word, He will supply our needs." God brought the same promises of His care to me in those hours of loneliness and decision.

David and I had known Kevin wanted to go to the mission field. I would miss him, but God could have him, and God would provide for us at home in the USA.

Two weeks before he left, orders for signs started coming in. By the time Kevin left, we knew we would have a busy summer making signs. Income would be adequate. God, my Provider, amazed me again. The abundance we saw that summer far surpassed our need.

God did not take care of me because
I am a widow, but because of His Word.

Why did I question God?

He Gave Me So Much

Philippians 4:19-23

"What you need is a little clinic in the backyard," Eli said.

"I think you're right," I agreed. I had just ushered the last patient out the door. Now I rinsed hypodermic syringes in the sink and put them into a pan to boil. "That would be better than treating sick people in our kitchen," I said, lining up the containers of gauze, tape, and cotton on the little table beside the refrigerator and covering it with a clean cloth. "But what about the money? How much would a little building cost?"

"Oh, I think I could build a little shack for about 50 dollars."

"Do you think God wants us to have a clinic?"

"Well," Eli answered, "we could find out. Let's pray and ask God to send us 50 dollars if He wants us to build a clinic."

Eli and I knelt. Almost hesitantly, we prayed, "Lord, if it is Your will for us to build a clinic, please send us 50 dollars."

Several days later, we received a letter. When we opened it, a check for 50 dollars fell out. It had been written before we prayed.

In the shower of funds that came in the weeks that followed, God showed us He is capable of giving us much more than 50 dollars. Eli built, not a little shack, but a two-room complex. We had enough money left to buy an examining table, a dentist chair, a small refrigerator, and all the medical equipment we needed.

Several years later, God provided funds that allowed us to move the clinic into a larger building. Since that first hesitant prayer 32 years ago, 32 thousand Salvadorans have received treatment in *Clínica Cristiana*.

Now when we need something, Eli and I approach with confidence the great Provider who is our Father. He showed us that He can give us much more than just 50 dollars. He never fails to supply all our needs.

Made Like Unto His Brethren

2 Corinthians 8:1-9

As Hurricane Mitch raged over Honduras, many Hondurans climbed onto dikes or up into trees. There they stayed for days. Fathers, mothers, children, and grandparents suffered from thirst and hunger. The next weeks they waded mud up to their thighs as they waited for the water to abate.

Two months later, our family and 14 others boarded a tugboat at Punta Gorda at 10:00 p.m. bound for the land whose people were still suffering from Mitch's ravages. It was a slow-moving vessel; the trip took eight hours. There was no rest room. At 3:00 in the morning a chilling rain began to mist our faces. We huddled under a leaky tarp. Women and children crowded into the cramped cabin.

Several days later one of the passengers spoke bitterly about the crossing. She felt she was still suffering from the inconveniences.

I was surprised. She knew we had tried to get a faster and more comfortable boat. As it was, she had had the most comfortable spot to sleep.

It was perplexing. We had come to serve a suffering people; people, who even now, were crammed into schoolhouses and sleeping on cold cement floors; people who were still wading through mud in their streets and houses; people who had loved ones fall out of trees and disappear into the cold, dark water. Couldn't we suffer a few hours of discomfort while others were facing weeks of hunger, homelessness, and sickness?

I turned my thoughts homeward. I, too, have complained of discomforts when I have had much for which to be thankful.

I turned my thought to Jesus. He became a man, suffering more than we have suffered and sparing Himself neither discomfort, danger, nor death. What great love and compassion! When my focus is on Him, my complaints are trivial and without merit.

God Is Good

Psalm 34:1-8

It was a terrific storm. Thunder, lightning, and rain! But our congregation was all safe and secure in the large campground auditorium. By dismissal time the sun was shining brightly. "Isn't God good!" "God surely blessed us to clear the storm by the time we dismissed." Such words echoed among the group. "Yes, God is good!"

I thought about it. What about the two-year-old killed last week when a gate fell on him? Was God good then? Is God good because of the good things that come our way? What about the bad things—deformities, disease, fire, rejection, and pain?

Our daughter died six weeks after open-heart surgery. I remember David and I visiting her in ICU following surgery. We were overcome by the tubes, cords, and monitors. She was aware of us. The second visit went better. Leaving her, we walked down the corridor and outside, softly singing, "God is so good. God is so good." She was recovering and our hearts rejoiced. Then came complications. A week later she died. Where was God then?

We learn a big lesson when we realize *God is good* even in the bad times. God is good no matter what happens. With Job we can say, "The LORD gave, and the LORD hath taken away; blessed be the name of the LORD" (Job 1:21).

In all that happens, we can still be carried in God's arms, protected from evil to our souls. We rightly praise God for the good times, but *we learn to know God* in the hard times.

Farewell, My Friend

John 15:9-17

*G*ood-bye, my friend.
Circumstances bid us part.
We've choices to make.
Time moves on. I'll always remember our
warm chats
Over coffee. How we shared!
We laughed, and we cried.
Although we'll keep in touch,
It will never be quite the same.
Farewell!

Good-bye, my friend.
Choices bid us part.
Our directions seem to be different.
Our interests have grown apart.
I'll never forget you. I'll pray for you.
If we never meet again, may we meet
up there
Where we can see as God sees.
Farewell!

Farewell, my friend.
Cancer has consumed your body.
Soon you'll be only a memory here,
But you will live forever—somewhere.
Be faithful to the end, dear friend,

lavished in God's grace.
I stoop to kiss you one last time.
Your weakened lips whisper—
Good-bye!

I turn and walk away with tears on my cheeks.
I ask God, "Why must I always part with
my friends?"
He whispers, "Child, you depend on them
too much.
Let Jesus be your Friend.
He can never be taken and
He all your needs can meet."

The song we sing so often,
I sing as never before:
Jesus is all the world to me,
My life, my joy, my all;
He is my strength from day to day,
Without Him I would fall.
When I am sad, to Him I go,
No other one can cheer me so;
When I am sad, He makes me glad,
He's my Friend.
Jesus is all the world to me,
I want no better friend;
I trust Him now, I'll trust Him when
Life's fleeting days shall end.
Beautiful life with such a Friend;
Beautiful life that has no end;
Eternal life, eternal joy,
He's my Friend.

-Will L. Thompson

As the Years Go On

Deuteronomy 8:1-5

*A*s a young girl, I remember thinking . . .
"When I'm older, my struggles will be few.
Life will level off and there will be an
evenness in my walk with the Lord.
I will reach a plateau, where there will
not be so much up and down, won't I?"

Well, now I am older. I have walked with God for several decades. And, surprise, I see no plateau. Though there are smoother stretches, there has been no leveling off.

I begin to understand the plight of Pilgrim in *Pilgrim's Progress*. Often his troubles came because of unwise decisions, and he suffered for them. Sometimes, however, his difficulties were tests from his heavenly Father.

Our Father has ways of getting our attention, causing us to see where our focus is, testing our dependence on Him and our love for Him. I see how my Father keeps bringing me back again and again to the three basic truths He was teaching me 12 years ago in the jungles of Central America. In those days of testing, I often felt I was only in God's kindergarten. Now, years later, I still often feel as if I haven't gotten past kindergarten. Yet, I realize the truths He keeps bringing me back to are not elementary. They are basic, foundational truths. They are truths that produce security. They are truths that help me *trust* Him. They are truths that help me *know* Him. And this is life eternal . . . that I may *know* Him!

These truths put a steadiness in my walk and will continue to be the foundation of my faith.

1. He is in control.
2. He makes no mistakes.
3. He is faithful.

CHAPTER TWO

"Let . . . the Wife . . . Reverence Her Husband"

Ephesians 5:33

What's Missing?

Ephesians 4:1-3, 15

*M*arriage seminars, marriage experts, and books on marriage all highly emphasize communication. They all tell us how and when to communicate, even where. We should know how to truly communicate by now, shouldn't we? But the divorce rate is higher then ever. What's missing?

Fifty years ago, there was emphasis on *commitment* and *contentment*. If they were strong in marriages today, they would balance with communication. Communication without commitment and contentment produces a struggle with expectations. Commitment and contentment enhances communication.

Commitment to my husband means I have an intense loyalty to our relationship. It is a determination to work together through any odds or incompatibility or hurdles. It is affirming to each other that divorce is never an option, that we are together for life. It is telling each other that if we could do it over, we would choose each other again. It is a decision to make our marriage work.

Contentment is acceptance of my husband as he is. Contentment is living together with a grateful spirit. It is not trying to change my mate. It is displaying a spirit of reverence and respect. It is giving up my rights, and yielding my expectations every day. It is forgiving one another.

I want commitment and contentment to be a foundation in our marriage. On that foundation we can build meaningful communication.

Our daily choices make a difference in our marriage. The choice to be meek, to be long-suffering, to forbear, to keep unity, lays the foundation for commitment and contentment.

So help us, Father....

Praying With My Husband

Philippians 4:4-7

*H*ow can a married couple keep from drifting apart? Often we are in contact with different people, do different things, and have different concerns. So, how do we keep love alive? How can we prevent communication breakdowns? Eli and I found one of the answers—praying together as a couple.

We made several attempts before we found a time that was right for us. When we prayed too late at night, or too early in the morning, our minds were groggy, and we had to struggle to stay awake. If we waited until after breakfast, we had too many interruptions. Finally, we started praying before breakfast. It worked. We may need to adjust our prayer schedule as our family changes, but the important thing is that we discovered what works for us now.

My prayer time with Eli meets a need that cannot be met by my personal devotions or our family worship. Praying together as a couple promotes understanding, fosters closeness, and helps communication. We pray about things we would hesitate to mention in the presence of the whole family. It helps us work through our differences, restores damaged relationships, and gives us peace in times of crisis.

Daily prayer with my husband brings me closer to him and to God. It is time well spent.

Communicate! #1

1 Corinthians 13:1-7

*M*arriage is communication. A lifetime of it!
What do we talk about? There are ordinary things to talk about. How was your day? Did you get that project finished? Tell something funny that happened. Share that verse that impressed you and that story that struck a chord in your heart.

Open up and share what's on your heart. It may be an inspiration or a goal you've set. Or perhaps you sense something is wrong, but you can't lay your finger on it. I have struggled with the latter, telling myself I shouldn't feel negative. I prayed and tried to overcome, but I didn't tell my husband. That was when I wanted to be the "perfect wife." I didn't want him to know the real me and the struggles I had. How foolish! There is beautiful freedom in openness and honesty. The "perfect wife" tells her husband how she feels and how things affect her. She needs his listening ear and kind help.

When you are upset, watch out! That may be the time to wait before you communicate. Be careful of overreaction and stretching the point. If you've been hurt by something he has said or done, let him know how you feel without accusing him. Try not to wear your feelings on your sleeve.

It has been said, "A true word kindly spoken will bring a man to reason quicker than a gallon of tears. Calm remonstrance is always better than weeping or moody silence. The first a man can understand; to the latter he has no key of interpretation."

Communicate! #2

1 Corinthians 13:1-7

*M*arriage is communication. A lifetime of it!
When do we communicate?
We need to find suitable times to communicate. Unloading the day's woes when your husband walks in the door after work is not wise. Then is the time to communicate love with a smile and a hug. Perhaps he's discouraged. A few loving words are so comforting. Learn to interpret his actions and gestures when he doesn't talk.

There are other unsuitable times. Maybe the children shouldn't hear, the phone rings, or you are just too weary. Table it for later. Dismiss it from your mind for now.

Find quiet, relaxed times to discuss weighty matters or things of the heart.

What about the times you can't agree on a major issue? An older woman shared this advice: "Be sure you are selfless, that you have an open mind, and a meek and quiet spirit. Understanding each other doesn't necessarily improve with time. We must keep working on it.

For finding solutions, what God says counts, not personal opinions. As wives, time alone with God in prayer and Bible reading is necessary preparation for each day."

The greatest blessing in marriage is coming to the Lord together. There we thank Him for His blessings and seek His help. Communication improves because we have communication with Him.

Little Things

Genesis 24:61-67

*M*y Dear Husband,
   I love you so much.
Your leadership in our home makes me feel secure.

You are kind and generous to everyone. Sometimes I have felt you are too generous, but why should I complain? I benefit more than anyone.

Your devotion to God and your faithfulness to Him in the choices you make inspire me. You make me want to be more devoted to Him too.

You are industrious, always busy. But in the middle of your busyness you show me that you care. I'll never forget the day in June when you stopped by the hayfield to check the hay. Before you got back in the truck, you stooped to pick a bouquet of bunny tails for me. They meant as much to me as red roses. I appreciate the big and obvious ways you show your love. But dear, I really believe it's the little things that build our relationship.

I want to look for *little* ways to return your love.

With Love,
Your Wife

A Lesson in Trust

Genesis 12:10–13:1

*M*y husband was asked to help plan a community event. Though he supported the project, the request did not come through our local church so he felt more free to decline. But I thought being involved would be a good idea, and I said so.

My husband was already over-committed and struggling to carve out some extras when this project came along. Though he tried to think of someone else, no one seemed to be available.

Whenever the subject came up, I politely hinted that perhaps he should accept the assignment. My comments fell on deaf ears. Though we didn't argue, I realized I'd said enough. It would have to be *his* decision.

I kept praying that God would give him wisdom to know if he should accept the responsibility.

Several weeks later, my husband sat in on the instruction class with our 14-year-old son. The minister taught how the Lord blesses us when we give of ourselves for others. If we withhold ourselves, God will withhold His blessing from us. That prompted my husband to trust God and accept the planning assignment.

This was also a lesson in trust for me. If I had pushed and pleaded, there would have been no blessing for either of us. Leaving it all to God left Him free to work. In trusting God I was free from worry and resentment.

Heavy Load, Grateful Spirit

Hebrews 13:15, 16, 20, 21

*A*ll of us have difficulty accepting some situations in life. As a doctor's wife, the demands of people on my husband, and indirectly on our family, have caused me great frustrations.

After we married and his practice was established, I realized this would be an uphill struggle for me. When family life was normal, I felt fine, but when my husband was gone night after night, I could hardly cope.

About 12 years later, God called my husband to the ministry. I now was also a minister's wife. In desperation, I cried to God for grace to accept this "heavy load." He gently showed me areas in my life I needed to change. My happiness had been dependent on circumstances, not on the Lord. I had been ungrateful. As I traveled on this journey to acceptance, a whole new outlook on life began to unfold. God gave me four keys to gratefully accept the "heavy load" He asked me to bear.

The first key to developing a grateful spirit is to realize all our benefits ultimately come from God. The second key is to lower our expectations of life, husband, children, friends, etc., by giving them to God. Our heavenly Father will meet our needs. The third key is to learn contentment with godliness by realizing that "things" compete with Christ. And the fourth key is to remember that all things work together for good. Remember God plans or permits everything that happens to us. Since He is totally sovereign, knows us completely, and loves us perfectly, we can trust Him without reservation.

Dear sister, are you struggling with a "heavy load" in your life? These keys will unlock the door to grateful acceptance.

Rest in Your Husband's Decisions

Ephesians 5:21-24

*W*hen a Central American church brother wanted to go to the States, my husband, Daniel, was asked to write a letter of recommendation. From the beginning, I questioned the wisdom of helping the brother this way. Today the matter came up again, so Daniel sat down to write the letter.

As I worked in the kitchen, my thoughts were as busy as my hands. Should I tell Daniel again how I felt about the matter? Finally, unable to keep silent any longer, I marched in to share my unsolicited advice.

Back at my work again, I felt justified in what I had done. Through the open doorway I could see my husband still seated before the typewriter, keys untouched. Suddenly, I was brought up short. What had I done? Had my well-meant words made it even more difficult for him to do what he felt he should?

I knew what I must do, and waiting would only make it harder. Humbly, I returned to his side and asked his forgiveness. I told him of my new resolve: "When I disagree with you, I will tell you how I feel, then leave it. I will pray that God will take your honest motives and use them as He sees fit."

The calm release and peace that followed far surpassed the momentary satisfaction of having things go *my* way. And since he is a Christian, I can be assured that Daniel will also take responsibility for the outcome of his choices. This is his God-given place and work. Mine, as his wife, is to stand by his side, supporting and submitting to him.

Yes, though, the battle of submission may have to be fought over and over within me, by keeping close to the Author of Order, I can be victorious.

An Hireling

John 10:11-18

*M*e? A hireling?

A beggar at the door had just asked me why I was discouraged. My honest answer had been, "Because you come so often."

As a missionary wife, I am constantly faced with the challenge of encouraging the heart of my shepherd husband by matching it with the heart of a shepherdess. Too often I fail, discouraging him and hindering his work by displaying the attitude of a hireling.

What's the difference?

A hireling endures the sheep, doing just enough to satisfy them so they don't bother her. She waits to be asked for food. A shepherdess loves the sheep, giving herself in deeds of kindness and compassion to all. She says, "You must be hungry. Let me get you something to eat."

A hireling does only what is expected of her, watching out for her own interest and safety. She says, "They can sleep on the couch; I will not have her and her messy children in the clean guest room." A shepherdess does more than is asked of her, caring thoughtfully about the comfort and soul peace of another. She, in remembrance of the Good Shepherd's sacrifice, cheerfully prepares clean, sweet-smelling beds even for those who bring lice with them.

When I have the heart of an hireling, it shows in my relationship with my husband too. The feeling of being "hired" into his ministry causes me to burn out emotionally and hinders the shepherding of my husband.

What joy I experience in being a shepherdess. What freedom I find in looking eagerly for ways to serve others. What peace of spirit I enjoy in putting others' needs before my own.

True fulfillment comes as I stand at the side of my shepherd husband, willingly sharing his burdens.

Used by permission of Sharon Eby.

I Need a Fortress

Psalm 18:1-6

I needed David this week. Sleep came more easily after talking with him about my fears and frustrations. But David is gone. Without my fortress, where do I turn? I still need someone to sound off to and help me, as a woman, to think through things. My mind just does not function as a whole.

My problem this week involved guarding my son. A new boy makes my son uncomfortable. This 15-year-old lies, cheats, and is disrespectful. He wants to spend time with my son, but we are disturbed. Where do I sound off my fears without being thought harsh, critical, unreasonable, or over-protective? Before, David and I would talk and seek God's way. But where do I go now?

I have learned that God is my first and reasonable source. He listens to me and knows how I long to guide and guard my son. As I brought this matter to the Lord, the Holy Spirit comforted me and gave me a sense of security for the night. Early the following morning, I placed the situation in Uncle Daniel's hands. I feel safer now regarding the matter.

Thank You, Lord, for not forsaking the fatherless and widow or single parent. Help us know when to carry our burdens to someone outside our homes. Help us to find that person from whom we can receive good counsel. As much as we want to function as a normal family, we are still lacking. Yes, Lord, help us. Be our Fortress and stronghold in the day of trouble. Our problems are too big for us.

CHAPTER THREE

"He Maketh . . . (Her) to Be A Joyful Mother"

Psalm 113:9

A Baby, Now?

Psalm 127

*Y*ou're gaining weight." I remember the spot where I was standing when I realized I could be pregnant. For days I protested to the Lord. How could He let this happen when I was dressing, bathing, shaving, and sometimes feeding, my husband David? When every letter he wanted written had to be dictated to me? How could I homeschool? Didn't God realize I had given away all my maternity clothes after Melissa was born five years ago? Didn't He remember I was 42 years old?

The most difficult question and one that resurfaced continually was, "What will my friends think?"

That question turned out to have the easiest answer. They told me. Some were shocked. Some were sympathetic. Some gave advice for the future. One cried because she had only three children and couldn't have any more.

Then there were those who rejoiced and encouraged me. They were enthusiastic about God's plans for this little one He had chosen to give us. They shared His vision of another blessing in our home. They helped me realize that just as we hold out our hands to friends and receive earthly gifts with gratitude, so we stretch our arms to our heavenly Father and say, "Thank You for Your gift."

The gift may be wrapped in aches and pains, extra effort, and added stress, but it is a good gift. Kenneth came. He is a joy and delight to us. We anticipate discovering the purposes God has for his life.

A Beautiful Present

Matthew 18:1-5

After my husband delivered our sixth child, we examined the perfectly formed body, counted the toes and fingers, and even noted the curly hair. Cuddling her, he nuzzled her cheek and murmured to me, "A gift from the Lord."

Yes, indeed, each of our eight children has been a wonderful gift from the Lord. Psalm 127:3 suggests that children are God's reward. "Lo children are an heritage of the Lord: and the fruit of the womb is His reward." Tragically, our world looks at children as nuisances, often killing them before they are born. Many are battered and emotionally abused. If only children could be viewed as His reward, as precious gifts.

Have you ever thought of your child as a beautifully wrapped present from God? A little girl asked a father of 12, "Mister, why do you have so many children?"

After thinking a bit, the father replied, "Tell me, do you like receiving only one birthday present or do you like many things? You see, the Bible tells us that children are a reward, or a present, from the Lord. My wife and I are enjoying lots of presents from God."

Dear mother, the next time you wipe that runny nose or change that dirty diaper, remember that God has blessed you with a special gift.

Longing for Motherhood

Psalm 113:1-9

*Y*ou long to become pregnant, to carry a baby in your womb. As a little girl, you looked forward to marriage and motherhood. You played with your dolls in anticipation. But your dreams are unfulfilled; your prayers are unanswered. You wonder "why?" You grieve for the child that has not been given to you.

One of the deepest pains of a woman is the unfulfilled longing to be a mother. God designed our bodies to bear children. Each monthly cycle is a preparation for pregnancy. When a woman waits in hopeful anticipation, and nothing happens, she may become frustrated and depressed.

I can identify in a limited way. I was privileged to have two children. But I longed for more. I had dreamed of a large family. I remember anticipation and disappointment. I struggled with stabs of jealousy as my friends became pregnant. I remember the overwhelming longings in my heart as I watched them care for their newborn babies.

Psalm 113:9 tells us, "He maketh the barren woman to keep house, and to be a joyful mother of children." I believe God wants to use each of our mother hearts to bring love and security to some child, whether born to us, or another woman's child that needs love and care. We can find healing for our longing hearts as we submit to God's direction for our lives and homes.

Our Own

Galatians 4:3-7

*H*ow many children do you have?"
   "We have four," I replied.
She stared curiously, then asked—
   "How many are your own?"
"We have four of our own,"
   I quietly affirmed.
"Two by birth, two by adoption;
      each one lent to us by God
         for a season,
      to teach, to train, and love,
      and then to release back to Him!"

Ours by birth or by adoption;
   rights and privileges
      all the same—
ours to provide and care for
   while we live on earth!

Whether by birth or by adoption,
   children may bring grief to parents.
But they need the assurance
   of belonging,
      even at their worst.
Young hearts are, oh, so tender;
   how they need to know
      they belong.

Their parents have chosen them,
    by birth or by adoption!
Thoughtless words so lightly spoken;
    "How many are your own?"
cause little hearts to wonder,
    "Do I belong?"
We are all adopted children,
    chosen by God for His very own—
It brings a great assurance,
    to know that we belong!

Keeping Our Children's Hearts

Malachi 3:16-18; 4:5, 6

To keep the hearts of our children
    is a priority;
  for if we have their hearts,
    we will have their loyalty,
      their respect,
        their obedience,
          and their honor.

If we have their hearts,
  we will invest time
    to listen to them,
    to disciple them,
    to teach them diligently,
    to understand and speak their love languages,
  and to pray with them.

To keep their hearts,
  we will invest in prayer
    for daily protection
  from that which can steal their hearts—
    friendship,
      activities,
        things,
          books,
            music.

Yes, it's an investment
　　and a full time job
　　to keep the hearts
　　　of our children.
For if we lose their hearts,
　　seeds of rebellion take root.
But if God has their hearts
　　　and we keep their hearts,
　　then their hearts
　　　will be turned
　　　　toward us
　　　and toward home.

Mud Pies or Rosebuds?

Deuteronomy 31:9-13

*O*ur little granddaughters were busy making mud pies as I prepared supper. I stepped out on the deck to watch their play. Four-year-old Ericka cheerfully presented me with a mud pie she had made. It was artistically decorated with candles, leaves, and two beautiful rosebuds. Several more buds were lying on the table. A closer look confirmed my suspicion. The rosebuds had come from my prized rosebush. I had anticipated these beautiful roses sitting in a vase on the dining room table.

As I looked at Ericka's shining blue eyes, I knew the roses were more important on the mud pies than in a vase. I thanked her for the gift and gently reminded her to pick flowers from the woods for her next pies.

As I thought about this incident, God showed me that grandchildren are more important than any possessions. I will give the gift of time and friendship to our grandchildren. They need my love and acceptance. I will try to pass on my values and convictions from God's Word. His Word tells us to teach our children and grandchildren His ways. Grandchildren need to respect our possessions, but they also need to know they are more important than rosebuds.

Love Without Partiality

Genesis 25:28 & 27:6-17

*D*avid and I hurt keenly. Death had taken our nine-year-old daughter.

After heart surgery, complications had set in, and five weeks later she died. We knew before surgery there was a chance we could lose her. After asking God's direction and discussing it with the doctors and others, we agreed to surgery. Evelyn was eager, because that was her nature. She wore her white dress to the hospital, to look like a nurse. She was excited. She loved adventure. She loved people. Looking back, it helps to know she felt that way.

But the loss, the void, was so consuming. We hurt deep inside.

Then while we were dealing with the loss, we heard the criticism, "David and Miriam loved Evelyn more than their other children." We were stunned.

David and I knew partiality can destroy a family. The Bible account of Isaac and Rebekah and their sons is a disturbing example. Because Jacob loved "Joseph more than all his brethren, they hated him." We did not want that. We wondered if our grief was exposing partiality in us.

We concluded that each child needs to be loved individually. Parents are to love each child deeply and truly. That is God's plan and a child's right.

Our grief at losing Evelyn included dealing with our attachment to her and our hopes for her future. It takes time to let go of a love relationship. We would never regret that we loved her so.

But did we love her more than the others? We finally asked our oldest daughter. "No," she answered. Our hearts were reassured.

Only in our loss did we appear partial. It was a time of detaching ourselves from Evelyn's presence. We would grieve as much for any of our children. We love them all—more now than ever.

Mother Comfort

Isaiah 66:10-13

*I*n my early childhood, I found a deep sense of comfort in Jesus. Yet I was so little acquainted with the God of all comfort. I used to wonder how that could be. Later I realized why.

It was Mom! When I would come crying, tears came to her eyes. In sickness, though we did not enjoy her home remedies, she comforted us.

As teens we would say, "Aw, Mom, go to sleep," when she poked her nose out of the bedroom door and asked, "Is everyone in now?" We'd be amused or annoyed at her concern, but still—there was a comfort knowing how much she cared.

Once, after a late shift in the hospital, I was on my way home at midnight. The night in front of me was black and deserted after the glare of city lights. I came upon a car going slowly and passed it. I could see a man at the steering wheel. A few moments later, he passed me and slowed down again. I had to press the brake. My adrenalin began pumping. What would I do at the stop sign ahead? I made sure the doors were locked.

At the intersection he turned the other way. Without stopping, I swung north, heading home. But the other driver made a swift U-turn and sped after me. I was terrified. If I could only get home! As the speedometer climbed to 90 m.p.h. I prayed and sang, "If ever I loved Thee, my Jesus, 'tis now," to calm myself.

I flew in our driveway, abandoned the car, and dashed to

the door. I knew Mom left it unlocked. From the safety of my home, I watched my pursuer drive slowly by.

As Mom stepped out of her bedroom door, I burst into tears and threw myself into her comforting arms.

"You are as white as a sheet," she said. "What happened?"

It was a relief to tell it all. Comforted, I dried my tears and headed for bed. Before I turned in, I reached for my Bible to acquaint myself more deeply with the God of all comfort.

On Being Mother and Father

Psalm 68:3-5; Jeremiah 49:11

*M*y son, Dwight, has been having car trouble. It finally seemed serious enough Monday that he took it to the garage. Last evening the garage man issued the verdict: a blown motor.

Disheartening news. Now what? Fix it? Get another car? Another motor? How much money shall I spend? How does one decide?

I wished Dwight had a father to discuss it with. But David is gone, and what good does my thinking do him? Listening? Yes, but my good sense doesn't go far on that subject. I did as I have learned to . . . I told him to talk it over with God, who is his Father, and He will direct him.

In a similar situation, Dorothy Hsu wrote this poem.

Mother and Father
On my knees I cried to You, Lord,
"Help! Please help me.
I'm trying to be both a mother and father
To my girls,
And I can't handle it. I'm failing."
Kindly, and gently, You responded
"Yes, you're a mother.
But no, You're not a father.
I'm the 'Father of the fatherless,'
I'll help you be a mother.
But you let me be the Father."*

I've often found courage in that message from God. I tell my children, "Ask God. He said He'll be a Father to you."

Repeatedly I have witnessed God's tender care for my children. Today I prayed to our Father as I went about my work. I prayed that He would guide my son in deciding about his car repairs.

Dwight checked at auto parts stores. He conferred with the mechanics. This evening he feels safe in the steps to take. We trust. We rest in our Father.

*Used by permission of the author.

Queen of the Home

Titus 2:1-5

*I*t was a balmy, fall afternoon, and I was working outside on a sign. Around the shop came a little boy almost dragging his school bag. I recognized him as my neighbor's great-grandson, a third or fourth grader.

After we exchanged greetings, he said, "Granny's not home. I was to get off the bus there. I've looked everywhere, but no one is there. Would you take me home?"

"I'll be glad to," I said, dropping my work. We hopped in the van and were soon at his house. But his mother wasn't home either! The anguish in his face said, "No one is home, and no one cares about me." He felt betrayed and forsaken. I learned later the mother had made other arrangements, but someone forgot to do his part. This incident reminded me of the sad state of affairs in many homes with absentee moms.

God calls mothers to be "keepers at home." My children want to know I'll be here when they return from school. If I'm not, they want to know ahead of time where I will be and what the plans are. I remember David wanted me home when he returned from work too.

HOME is where mom is Queen. It is not to be a cage for mother, but her realm of service. It becomes our "Motherhood" to make the house a *HOME* by being present, and pleasant, for our families, to make home the most comfortable place in the world for those who belong there.

The Proverbs-31 Woman

Proverbs 31:10-31

I feel overwhelmed every time I read this passage. This woman has it all together. Talk about wonderful character qualities and accomplishing much, this is it!

How can I be this virtuous woman? I want my children to call me blessed and my husband to praise me. I desire to be a woman of excellence. How can I achieve these goals of providing for my family and reaching out to others when I am only a homeschooling mom of eight children? The workload is unbelievable. Sometimes I cannot even prioritize; there are too many things of equal importance. I must go to the Source of true virtue, God, my heavenly Father. I must keep the goals before me, working on a few areas at a time.

Wise and kind – *She openeth her mouth with wisdom; and in her tongue is the law of kindness* (verse 26). Wisdom and kindness go hand in hand. Wisdom is reflected in our choice of words. Kindness is shown in our tone of voice.

Observant – *She looketh well to the ways of her household, and eateth not the bread of idleness* (verse 27). My children think I have eyes in the back of my head! Being observant involves knowing what goes on in their lives.

Merciful – *She stretcheth out her hand to the poor; yea, she reacheth forth her hands to the needy* (verse 20). A poor person is lacking in something. It could be a young family with a newborn that needs a meal brought in.

Active – *She girdeth her loins with strength, and strengtheneth her arms* (verse17). Who supplies the energy and stamina for the job? It is the Lord. *He giveth power to the faint; and to them that have no might he increaseth strength* (Isaiah 40:29).

Noble Character – *Who can find a virtuous woman? for her price is far above rubies?* (verse 10). A woman of excellence is rare in today's world of "liberated" working women.

A Mother's Prayers

Psalm 55:16-18, 22

God sees the young mother
    busy with her little ones,
    the baby in the cradle,
    the toddlers at her feet.
God knows the toil, the thankless tasks
    waiting to be done.
    He understands her longings,
    her need for a quiet time
      alone with Him.

So He gives her opportunities.
    When the toddlers are asleep,
    she sits in her rocking chair,
    the baby at her breast,
  her Bible open on her lap,
    pouring out her heart
      to God.
Or she wakes early in the morning
    while the family is fast asleep.
    It is her time alone with God.
    She is refreshed.

The children are playing happily,
    so she kneels beside her bed.
    The little ones find her there,
    and she draws them down beside her.
    They learn to be silent
        before God.

God sees the young mother;
    He knows her longings,
    the deep desire in her heart
    for a quiet time alone
        with Him.

And so He reaches down
    and gives her renewed
    strength and grace
    for her duties
        for today!

The Wise Woman

Proverbs 14:1, 2 and Matthew 5:3-9

*E*very wise woman buildeth her house . . ."
How?

She builds with the law of kindness on her tongue,
speaking life
and blessing
and praise
to her family.

She builds by demonstrating
a meek and quiet spirit,
that is, a gentle, undisturbed,
and an unruffled spirit.

She builds by honoring and respecting her husband,
doing him good
and not evil, all her days.

She builds her house
by fearing the Lord.

"But the foolish woman plucketh it down with her
hands."
How?
By criticism
impatience
speaking words of death to her children,
instead of words that give life.

The foolish woman tears down
    by demonstrating
        fear and anger
            instead of meekness and quietness.

She tears down
    by dishonoring
        disrespecting
            and criticizing her husband
    and by displaying a lack
        of admiration
        and trust in him;
    by not building up
        the father image in the home.

Father, pour wisdom into me
    and make me a true
        and sincere
            builder of my house.

Away With Fretfulness!

Psalm 37:1-7

*M*y heart yearns over my children. I love them. I care so much. Sometimes I am anxious and fearful; I worry, fret, and criticize. I police their words and actions, and pronounce judgment upon them. Trying to make sure nothing slips by me leaves me nervous and constantly nagging. There have been times I "righteously" corrected a situation only to find I had passed judgment before I knew the facts. My critical analysis inspires more negative behavior. Counter-productive? Very!

Yes, there's a lot of effort on my part, but also an uncomfortable awareness of failure. I pray hurriedly and blunder on. (I must take care of things, they've got to learn!). But I haven't stopped, or waited, to hear counsel.

How tense I am! What a contrast to the peace and calm I once knew. This agitated spirit has churned up troubled waters—waters I had hoped to calm with the oil of peace. In humility I come to God for help.

Lord, I love these precious children, but I realize Your love for them is perfect. I shall rest in Your love. I shall relax; not without concern, but trust. I commit them to You, Lord. I know You are working in their lives; therefore I can joyfully do my part. Away with fretfulness!

Thank You for 'remembering my frame.' May I pass on the favor to my children? They are children, and they are learning. May I be alert without being jumpy? Make me wise to encourage and nurture them, as well as restrain and correct them.

Father, this calling to motherhood is dear to my heart. You have placed children in our home, a precious trust! I bring their lives and our home relationships to You for Your blessing.

Lord, I shall be renewing this prayer and commitment to You often. I'm so human, that's why Your grace is such a blessing. Thank You for the sweet comfort of knowing You, my Source of wisdom. Amen.

Feeding My Family

Proverbs 14:1; 24:3-5

*N*o question about it, getting good, nutritious food on the table on time is a challenge. The responsibility falls squarely into my lap. Failure can be far-reaching. Simple, well-balanced meals enjoyed together help all of us function better.

On the other hand, providing ample spiritual food and time to consume it is my husband's responsibility. But wait! Am I making it easy for him to carry out this awesome task? Can I do anything to give him more time and energy to teach our children?

Without being aware of it, we can put pressure on our husbands that chokes their desire and makes opportunities for family devotions harder to come by. For example, could feeding our household be easier if I didn't demand such high living standards? Am I spending time or money on things that are not *really* important?

How about a quick inventory of my attitude? Do I fully support our *family altar*? Family devotions should be unhurried so that there is time for questions and discussion. *Mealtime* also needs evaluation. Am I doing my part in preparing meals on time so that this time together can be an informal time of teaching and sharing? Cozy winter *evenings at home* that lend themselves to discussion and togetherness are invaluable. Children are often quite open at *bedtime* if there is time to chat and pray. Limiting evenings away from home may not be easy, but it may be part of the key to togetherness.

I want to be faithful in providing nourishing food for my family and in assisting my husband in feeding the family spiritually.

What Am I Teaching?

Psalm 37:27-40

*S*omeone did my child a bad turn. He was hurt and angry. "Why, I'd like to . . . ," he fumed, describing how he would retaliate. I sympathized. I would have enjoyed teaching the offending brat a thing or two myself!

The conversation got out of hand as the other children joined in thinking up ways to get even. Nothing really bad, but "it would serve him right" nonetheless.

Suddenly it hit me. How can I expect my children to grow up and return good for evil when deep down, I don't. Oh, sure, I say I do, but a close examination of the thoughts and intents of my heart shows a lack.

Convicted, I asked God to forgive me. My quick temper does not help. Though I still struggle, I am trying.

We must be careful for our words and actions influence our children. Is it spiritually upbuilding to them to tell of our escapades as children—especially getting back at someone who wronged us? It can be upbuilding if they are told in the right spirit for the right purpose. Our children need to know we are sorry for what we did. Such tales should not be told for entertainment. I must help my children see Jesus' perfect standard of love. It goes against the grain, but we must teach our children nonresistance.

If Vernon and I don't teach them, who will?

Lord, the next time someone wrongs a child
of mine, help me to respond as a child of Yours,
to model forgiveness as Christ forgave.

Suns or Clouds?

Proverbs 10:19-21, 31, 32

*T*he decision was made. José,* who was from another part of the country, was coming to spend some time with us. He was the only Christian in his family, and he needed work. My husband had kindly decided to help him out by letting him come for several weeks.

Unknown to me, our oldest daughter, Julia, was apprehensive about how I would respond. She knew I didn't like the idea. "Will Mama give José the 'cold shoulder' treatment?" she wondered. Later, Julia shared her feelings with me, including the relief she felt when I calmly accepted José into our home.

God had helped me accept his coming, to be kind when he arrived, and yes, even *enjoy* his stay with us. What a blessing José was when, a few days after his arrival, my husband fractured his leg.

Another day a lady was at the door. Her voice was demanding and loud. Julia answered the door, but the lady wanted to see me. Again, Julia was afraid of how I might respond. She was relieved when I didn't become upset.

My eyes were opened. May I never forget. *Our children sense our attitudes and are very much affected by them.* Mothers, it is like sunshine in their day when we are happy and calmly accept interruptions. But it is a chilling fog when we become upset and carry our unhappiness with us.

Oh, to be a sun, not a cloud! And when hard times come, that our children may see us leaning hard on God.

*Name changed.

Become as Children

Mark 9:35-42

I felt myself a failure as a mother. I saw so few results for all my efforts in corrective discipline. We've been working a long time on "do your work promptly, cheerfully, and diligently."

Today was a little different. I believe I learned something. It was *not* successfully checking things off my "to do" list. We served hot lunch at our church school. It took all morning to prepare. The three preschoolers and I stayed for the story-time after lunch for the special feeling of going to school with big sister.

In the afternoon, I helped big sister build a sandcastle such as I used to make, complete with flowers. When the cool sand was well packed around my bare feet, I could pull them out, leaving a hollow basement as good as any I ever made in childhood.

The twins were pleased when I drew a horse for them to embroider. But that also meant threading needles and untangling unwanted knots all afternoon.

Just before Daddy came home for supper, I called an alarm for the whole crew to pick up toys and tidy the living room. I was amazed at how promptly, cheerfully and diligently it all got done. Somehow I didn't make the connection until Daddy wisely observed, "It's fun to work for Mama when she takes time to play with us."

Except ye become as little children, ye shall not usher your children into the kingdom.

Your Mission Field
at Home

Mark 10:13-16

*S*ometimes I feel a restlessness in my spirit. The mundane tasks of changing dirty diapers and teaching math concepts over and over are exhausting. Guiding my teens is overwhelming at times.

I look beyond my world to the challenges of a counseling ministry never developed. The vision for a community ladies' Bible study never materialized. As a pastor's wife, I see unmet needs in our congregation. There is so much to be done.

What exactly is my mission? I was pondering this question when an older, but wiser woman replied, "Your mission field is at home, dear."

The Cry of the Mothers

My life is so narrow, so narrow;
Environed by four bare walls,
And ever across my threshold,
The shadow of duty falls.
My eyes wander oft to the hilltops,
But ever my heart stoops down
In a passion of love to the babies
That helplessly cling to my gown.

In the light of a new day dawning,
I see an evangel stand,
And to the fields that are white to harvest,

He lures me with beckoning hand;
But I have no place with the reapers,
No part in the soul-stirring strife.
I must hover my babes on the hearthstone.
And teach them the lessons of life.

But at night when the lessons are ended
And I cuddle each sleepy head,
When the questions are asked and answered
And the last little prayer has been said;
When the fruitless unrest has vanished
That fretted my soul each day,
Then I kneel in the midst of my children
And humbly and gratefully pray:

"Dear Lord, when I stand with the reapers,
Before Thee, at set of sun—
When the sheaves of the harvest are garnered
And the labor of life is done—
Let me lay at Thy feet these, my children;
To my heart and my garment they cling.
I cannot go forth with the reapers,
Yet these are the sheaves that I bring."

This poem is a selection from *Heart Throbs of Motherhood*, a book available from Share-A-Care Publications, 240 Mohns Hill Rd., Reinholds, PA 17589. Used by permission.

A Gift for a Lifetime

Proverbs 23:12-15

A pastor visited a home where rowdy boys were misbehaving. "It's a stage all boys go through and eventually outgrow," the father commented.

Wait a minute! Do children who are allowed to disobey, throw tantrums, and show disrespect to their parents grow out of it? I have seen adults behave the same way in the church, in a more dignified manner, of course.

One of the greatest gifts I can give my children is a proper respect for authority. It is a gift for a lifetime. Children taught to respect their parents' authority will then willingly submit to the authority of their teacher, church leader, and ultimately God. The gift of submission allows our children to more easily accept Christ as their Saviour. Picture Christ knocking at the door of your child's heart, asking to come in and take control of his life. If your child has not learned to submit to your authority, it will not be easy for him to accept Christ as Lord of his life.

In my quest for total acceptance of my role as a doctor-minister's wife, I have wished I had received more spankings as a child. Yes, there were times I rebelled in a dignified manner, but inwardly I was hitting the walls in frustration. Can an adult throw a tantrum? I am ashamed to say I have. I well remember throwing the phone after an especially frustrating week with my husband gone night after night and our plans changed one more time. Perhaps, if I had not grown up so self-willed, giving control of my plans to God would have been easier.

Young mother, teach your little ones to submit. It is one of the greatest gifts you can give your children, one that will last a lifetime.

Train Up a Child

Proverbs 22:6; 29:15-18

*S*everal of us were visiting outside after church last evening, when suddenly, a three-year-old dashed away from his mother. She chased him saying, "You come back here. You aren't to go to the creek." The child was drawn back, but only moments later darted toward the road. The reprimand was repeated.

Seeing this made me wonder. Will the parents get a hold of this, or will the child always be leaping at danger, knowing a heavy hand will draw him back? Will there be consequences for disobedience? Will he learn subjection to his parents? Will he be taught the blessing of boundaries? This child *is* being trained but not wisely.

I see another picture; a willful child becomes a teenager and a young adult, resisting parents, resisting the law, or authority in general, then a strong hand drawing him back. He still hasn't learned. How sad. What will his end be?

Sometimes willful youth from Christian homes come to Christ, still resisting. They resist the church leaders and guidelines, hardly aware they are resisting God and His Word. Other undisciplined youth turn away from God altogether, following their selfish desires to destruction. How tragic!

Proverbs 22:6 says, "Train up a child in the way he should go: and when he is old, he will not depart from it." Good training or poor, he will find it hard to turn from his training.

How am I training my children? Have I allowed begging,

talking back to parents, resisting commands, lying, delayed "obedience," cheating, arguing, or half-done jobs in my children? Left untended now, these patterns will be difficult to change later. The verse says, "Train up a child," which means diligently building character traits while he is young and teachable. Let's have the foresight to teach our children with loving, firm discipline so they can eventually guide their own steps, having learned self-discipline.

Of Tending Sheep and Killing Giants

Matthew 25:14-23

*I*n a penetrating sermon last weekend, the preacher said David's youth can be summed up in two parts: tending sheep and killing giants. We simply can never do great things such as killing giants unless we have first faithfully tended our sheep. That thought kept coming back. Tending sheep and killing giants. Hmm . . . It *is* important that I do faithfully what God has called me to. It may not look as if I am accomplishing much as a mother, but there is more to the story.

All around us we are seeing the results of mothers failing to do their jobs. Prisons are filled with "handicapped" people who have never learned to function normally in society. Day care centers are filled with unhappy children who are missing their moms. Many of them feel insignificant and worthless.

We may rarely place our children in the care of others, but if we long for freedom from the responsibilities of home, we are missing the mark. Being a loving and faithful mother is a most important way to tend sheep. Faithful mothers will someday be richly rewarded with gifts that cannot be bought. Those who faithfully "tend sheep" may also be called upon to "kill a giant!"

This Thing Called Time

Psalm 90

*T*his thing called TIME
      is a constant juggle
     for a mom
     like me.

Every day I have opportunities
    to choose between
      the urgent and the important.

My windows need cleaning (that is urgent),
    but my son is begging me to sit down with him
      and a favorite book (that is important).
    The windows will wait
      (that is availability).

The evening meal needs to be started (that is urgent),
    but my daughter is asking me to go
      on a walk with her (that is important).
    I'll change the menu and simplify the meal
      (that is flexibility).

The sewing . . . for five ladies in our house . . .
    when will I ever get to it (that is urgent)?
    But my baby needs cuddling.
      His "love tank" signals
        it needs filling again, and then again
      (that is important).

Meanwhile, we will wear what we have
(that is resourcefulness).

The house needs a good decluttering
and corners need organizing (that is urgent),
but my husband needs me to sit down with him
for a debriefing about our day
(that is important).
The clutter will not walk away
(that is sensitivity).

The porch windows need replacing (that is urgent),
but the children ask to go away
for a few days—for quality family time
(that is important).
The windows will hold back the cold
another season
(that is contentment).

The opportunities God gives me to choose between
the urgent and the important
are opportunities to cry out to Him
again and again
and again.

Time Management for Busy Moms

Ephesians 5:15-20

*H*ave you ever wished for more hours in a day? Would a 26-hour day really solve the problem? It seems I am always wishing for more time to finish my work.

When my husband got busier with his work and the ministry, and we began homeschooling our children, I knew we needed better time management in our home. I bought a plan book with yearly, monthly, and weekly pages to keep everything in perspective. I can see at a glance when my husband has commitments and can plan my work accordingly. This has helped us immensely.

Prioritizing is the key to successful time management. How does one prioritize when there are so many important things to be done? Here are some tips that have helped me prioritize:

Drop–

Simplify your life as much as possible. Prayerfully consider your plans, schedule, family, or church activities. Many times we do what appeals to the flesh. Think about how God looks at it. Using His wisdom, drop what is least important or is unproductive.

Delay–

Keep an eye on your list for items that could be delayed. This does not mean they are unimportant, but rather they can wait.

Delegate–

Ask your children to do more around the home, freeing you to do what needs your input and guidance. Sometimes we think we have to do everything or it won't get done right. Delegate! Allowing our children to learn work skills is much more important than perfect housekeeping.

Do–

Finally, after we have dropped, delayed, and delegated everything we can, we have left the important things to tackle. A little less to do will help us accomplish the important things in life and enjoy our families more.

Your Labor Is Not Futile

Isaiah 26:3-9

*I*t was the third and final day of Leaders' Conference. While the business meeting was in session, a number of us slipped away to the grand grocery and variety store a quarter mile away to buy or browse.

When it was time to return, Sara offered me a ride in her van. While we waited for a few more passengers, I noticed boys' shoes on the floor between the seats and commented on them.

"Yes, when the boys get in the van after church, they take them off. Sometimes the shoes stay in the van until the next Sunday," Sara said. Besides being a minister's wife in the church hosting these meetings, Sara is also mother of five children, four of them preschoolers.

Back at the church, Sara shared her struggles and the discouragement she felt in getting a family ready for church. "And then, when I finally sat down in church this morning, I didn't have my Bible!" she finished with tears in her eyes.

Sound familiar? Sometimes we wonder if the effort is worth it. Take courage, sisters, it is! God knows if our desire is to Him. He knows our motives as we come to His house, even though we've mislaid our Bibles, or little Susie's hair looks as if it was never combed, or Johnny's shirt tail is hanging out–again.

Let's not forget about the precious seeds we're sowing in our children's hearts as we take them to church with us. What an excellent way to show them what we hold most important in life! When the children are grown (though now you can't imagine it), and you see them choose God and become useful in His kingdom, you will know it was worth it all.

"Therefore, my beloved [sisters], be ye stedfast, unmoveable, always abounding in the work of the Lord, forasmuch as ye know that your labour is not in vain in the Lord" (1 Corinthians 15:58).

An Egg or a Scorpion?

Luke 11:9-12

*W*hich of you, if your child asks for an egg, will offer him a scorpion?

One afternoon Jennifer asked me to help find some photos for her album. I was about to say no and hurry on by when the question above flashed into my mind. I paused and thought. I could make time to fill her simple request.

As we dug out treasures for her project, I wondered at all the scorpions I had handed out in the past with a stinging, "too busy." I had denied my children's desire for the "nourishment" of my companionship, the pleasure of doing a small project together. The thought almost made me weep. My busyness had not been with great works but simply the everyday duties so important to mothers.

Now I have no regrets for the minutes we spent poring over forgotten memories . . . "Here's when you were a baby!" "Remember *that* trip through Mexico?" There are class pictures . . . and lots of birthdays and birthday cakes. It was a pleasure helping Jennifer choose the right pictures for her book. The satisfaction is a reward all its own. I have no regrets.

Yes, an egg nourishes, fills, and satisfies. A scorpion stings.

A Little Child Shall Lead Them

Matthew 18:1-5

I kept him home from school that day. After doing dishes and helping him begin some schoolwork at the kitchen table, I brought out my Bible and notebook.

"Son, you must be quiet. I didn't read my Bible this morning, so I want to read it now."

"What for?" he asked.

"I need it. It helps me do right."

"Oh, you mean when you get mad." He was satisfied that he understood.

Mad! Mad? Is that how he saw me when I was upset?

"Yes, son," I humbly admitted. "I need it when I get angry . . . and other times too."

That soul-searching arrow went straight to my heart. I had been edgy and easily upset and had been justifying myself as well.

Thank You, Lord, for using children to humble us and help us see ourselves before You.

Birthdays

Ephesians 1:3-6

I don't know what birthday traditions you have. Some families let the birthday V.I.P. take the first piece of cake, be it smack out of the middle, or with a sticky one-year-old fist.

In our family it is becoming a tradition to ask the birthday child what kind of a cake he wants. Children's imaginations are more vivid than mine. The twins' require two cakes, because they are individuals with distinct ideas. I am always a little apprehensive that my inventions will not meet their expectations. But somehow, no matter how lowly, they are tickled, and so am I, when I see their faces shining in the candlelight.

I think it has to do with being loved for who they are. There is no performance expected to earn this cake. There are no strings attached but Mama's heart strings. The birthday cake stands as a monument to their significance.

Today's birthday boy thinks Lego steps and a house on a round cake are wonderful. He seems to have forgotten his request that they be made of icing. The cake is forgotten because he senses he has received a greater gift: the security of his parents' special love and blessing. I need to find more ways to "bless" him before his next birthday.

Because He Lives

2 Corinthians 4:11-18

*D*ear Daughter,

When you were born, someone sent us the words to the song, *Because He Lives*. Its message assured us that the joy of a sweet newborn does not need to be clouded with uncertainties about an unknown future. Yes, we could face uncertainties with confidence, "Because He Lives."

That was 22 years ago. I imagined we might face persecution or financial hardship, end-time pestilence, or some dreadful disease such as cancer. I never thought of facing a parting like this. God has called you and your husband to be missionaries in Belize many miles from home. We will face lonesome days, poor and expensive telephone service, and terrible mail service. You may face tropical storms and sicknesses. If God blesses you with children, we'll miss seeing our grandchildren take their first steps or hearing them utter those first words. But Jesus lives, and we can face these days *because of Him.*

Love,
Mom

Let Go—Let God

James 4:1-8

*O*ur son had asked a girl about beginning a special friendship. Now he was waiting for her answer. After months of waiting, he received her answer, "No." My mother heart ached. "I'm praying that she will change her mind," I confided to a friend.

"Maybe you should pray that *he* will change *his* mind," she replied.

My first thoughts were, "You don't understand." But as I thought it over, I decided that was exactly what I would do.

Only a few months later, God miraculously brought another young lady into my son's life. She is now our very dear daughter-in-law.

Many times I look at my selfish hopes and think the way I have things planned is the way it must be. But when I commit the matter to God and submit to His plan, the pieces begin to fit together.

I ran across a quote the other day that says, "Curb your appetite to control events and people; otherwise you will be unhappy." I'd like to take that a step further and say, "Curb your appetite to control God's plans; otherwise you will be unhappy."

When our "almost" adult children are making decisions and our hearts ache, we must remember to let go, and let God work out the details.

Me? A Mother-in-Law?

1 Corinthians 13:4-7

*T*he prospect of becoming a mother-in-law frightened me. I had heard too many stories about mother-in-law/daughter-in-law conflicts. As our oldest son's wedding approached, I became increasingly fearful about my new role. I asked my friends to pray for me. They did, and God heard their prayers. He gave me a beautiful relationship with Bonnie.

A few years later, our second son married Bonnie's sister Judy. Now I have two daughters-in-law from the same family. Bonnie and Judy make our family more complete. We love and appreciate them very much.

The mother-in-law role, I believe, is just as subject to peril as any other relationship. The same rules of love and respect apply. I try to understand the difference between interest and interference, between being concerned and being controlling. I want to cultivate harmony and rapport with my daughters-in-law.

Ruth and Naomi demonstrated an exceptional bond between in-laws. Rooted in the common faith they embraced, it grew stronger with the passing years. What better proof of the spiritual caliber of a woman than the love she has for the wife of her son? What stronger evidence of her spiritual vigor than the way her daughter-in-law returns that love? Naomi gave an example for us women to follow. I want to learn from her to be a good mother-in-law.

Mother-in-Law

Ruth 1:1-10

*I*t's their second anniversary. And mine! Today it's two years that I stepped into these mother-in-law shoes.

At first I admired them—so shiny and new. I was privileged to have them. But as shoes can do, they gave me some blisters. Sometimes they pinched. They felt tight. Could I escape them?

No. Just as motherhood is a "forever" job, so is mother-in-law-hood!

The first two years are over, and I'm glad I didn't dispose of the shoes, or complain, or flee blisters and pinching. The shoes feel more comfortable now, but not nearly like old house slippers! They are still too shiny and new. But I have hopes that in a few more years, they will be as comfortable as motherhood shoes.

CHAPTER FOUR

"Be at Peace
Among Yourselves"

1 Thessalonians 5:13

To a Dear Friend

2 John

*D*ear friend of mine,
      I thank my God for you.
   You're constant
      thro' life's thick and thin,
         whether near or far.
   Tho' others change and bend as pressures come,
      you hold to values solid as the Rock.
You strengthen me by
   being who you are,
      and what you are,
         and being there.
How precious is your warm and caring spirit!
   Your heart is always open
      to another's burdens, cares, and tears.
   With warmth and love,
      you hold out comfort sweet.
I pray my God for you.
   You're human too,
      and need His help divine as well as I.
I pray you'll be faithful to the end,
   that in your daily walk
   you'll please our dearest Friend.
I'm drawn to God thro' you.
   I see His workmanship in you,
      His Living Word is part of you,
         His presence truly there.

You're walking hand in hand with Christ—
  That's where you learned such friendship true!
I'm looking forward
   to more times together here.
   We'll rejoice together,
    laugh a bit,
     and pour out our hearts.
But more, I'm looking forward to the Eternal Day
   when we can share and enjoy more fully
    with none of earth to hinder us.
Yes, rooted in the Timeless One,
   our friendship will not die and wither,
    but blossom fuller, sweeter,
     "Over There."

Hold a Friend With Two Hands

Romans 12:10-16

*S*he did it again. Regina willingly left her quilting project to care for my three preschoolers while I rushed off to the doctor—again. Though I resisted, I had to go back on medication for bipolar disorder. It was almost more than I could bear to stop for groceries after seeing the doctor. Could I hold myself together enough to pick up the children yet?

I found Regina sitting on the floor, reading to the boys. She helped James get his puppy box (with the puppy inside) and showed us where all the clothes and jackets were neatly organized by the door. By now, finding a lost shoe would have been too much for me to handle. We were ready to leave.

Then I saw a quilt in its frame. It was a baby quilt. I threw my arms around Regina and tried to thank her for being a sister in suffering. No words came.

She has no children of her own.

Comfort Is for Comforting

2 Corinthians 1:3-7

I thought I would have a "grief trip" returning to the North Carolina campground meetings this year. David had been along the last time I'd been there. My mind begged to taste the sweet sorrow of past memories. I knew it could hinder my joyful spirit. *But surely I have a right to grieve,* I thought to myself.

What I met were women hurting from griefs more fresh than my own. Some were hurting deeply for the cause of Christ.

Sally's husband wants her to compromise her convictions about living separate from the world. She tried going back to a church of his choice only to find her spiritual needs unmet.

To keep her peace with God, Rachel was forced to a marital separation. It was very painful to her. She was closed to talk, even when I told her I'd be praying for her. But when I told her my husband had died nearly four years before, she reached out and touched my arm, saying, "So you are single too."

Then she began to talk, but so softly I could hardly hear her.

As I communed with these women, I found my sorrow and loneliness bridging the gap to these hurting ones.

These Christian women needed courage pressed into their hands. Sally could see that trust is resting in God.

Rachel was hungry to know that loneliness can be endured. God will be her companion and steadfast hope.

I could pass on to them how God tenderly cared for my family. "Yes," I could say, "Sons need fathers, and we can help them trust our heavenly Father by being examples of faith. Yes, we need godly men to help in decisions. Seek God for that answer among the brotherhood."

This weekend was not a "grief trip" after all. With God as my comfort, my hurt subsided, and I was able to reach out to others.

"O, Sally and Rachel, may you find strength for your days, and some day you will comfort other weary ones."

Burdens and Balm

Isaiah 49:13-16

*N*ora's* husband isn't always considerate of her. Elaine* and her family are victims of a less-than-ideal church setting. My parents are aging, but I live 3,000 miles away and am unable to help, as I would love to.

How should I pray for these needs and many others like them? What could I say to make a difference? Often these burdens would weigh heavily on my heart even after I had prayed. We've all heard the saying, "Either you have a big God and a little problem, or else you have a big problem and a little God."

Finally, I went to the Book of books for a cure. I should have done it long before. I had endured a nagging ache long enough. I turned to 1 Peter 5:7, one of my favorites. The Amplified Bible says it like this: "Casting the whole of your care—all your anxieties, all your worries, all your concerns, once and for all—on Him, for he cares for you affectionately *and* cares for you watchfully." What a healing balm for hearts—theirs and mine! What's more, the supply is unlimited.

How to administer this tonic? "The Lord GOD hath given me the tongue of the learned, that I should know how to speak a word in season to him that is weary: he wakeneth morning by morning, he wakeneth mine ear to hear as the learned" (Isaiah 50:4).

Someone has said, "Wise counsel for the discouraged must come from God." As I stay close to Him, faithfully having daily devotions, I will have something to share that will make a difference.

Thank You, Lord, that You see the needs of all the Noras and Elaines. You have even promised to continue carrying the aged ones as You have from birth. Help me stay close to You so that I will have Your healing balm ready, available to spread to the needy hearts around me.

*Names changed.

What's the Use?

Galatians 6:7-10

*W*hat's the use trying to help these sisters? What good will my efforts do? I had visited Anita almost daily for weeks, but she and her husband still broke up. Sometimes I feel as if I didn't help at all.

Now a new problem has surfaced. Marlene says she hates Elva. It all started over a fight between their children. The little ones have forgiven and forgotten. They play together again as if nothing happened. But these two church members have not only kept quarreling, they have drawn others into their conflict.

*   *   *   *   *

Months later—

My heart warmed when I saw Marlene and Elva standing close together to sing a song. After church, Marlene told me, "Elva and I now love each other more than we ever did before. Thank you for helping us resolve our problems."

*   *   *   *   *

Now I ask—

Is it worth the effort to try to help my Christian sisters? Yes, it certainly is. Even in Anita's case, where things still aren't resolved, I want to be faithful.

Lord, make me an instrument of Your peace.

Vinegar and Oil
Relationships

Proverbs 15:1-4

I love Italian foods. Lasagna, pizza, stromboli, and spaghetti are favorites. These cheesy pastas are wonderful, accompanied with warm, crusty bread and a fresh, crisp, garden salad tossed with a favorite dressing. Mine is Italian, a zesty vinegar and oil combination.

What makes this dressing so flavorful? Is it the oil? Is it the vinegar or the spices? It is the blend. Since the vinegar and oil easily separate, one must always shake the bottle before using it. I have forgotten, and had an oily salad. Ugh! But, only vinegar makes my mouth pucker. No, they are best when blended together.

Did you know God uses a vinegar and oil dressing for relationships in the body of Christ? Eph. 4:15a refers to "speaking the truth in love." Truth in our communication is the vinegar; saying it with love is the oil.

Just as you must shake the dressing prior to use, so you must blend truth and love in your speech. I have used only vinegar and caused needless conflict. Conveying truth to individuals with sin in their lives may cause them to reject the truth because they felt no genuine concern. On the other hand, being the people pleaser I am, I have spoken with only oil. I was afraid of what people might think of me if I spoke the truth about their lives.

My friend, are you having problems in your relationships? Perhaps you are using too much vinegar. Or oil. Try using a blend of Biblical proportions.

How Well Do I See Me?

Romans 12:3-8

*P*ersonal relations and getting along with others takes God's help.

When my daughter sees a fault in a friend, she wonders when the girl will grow up. One complains, another is a "know-it-all," and Jane can't stand hard work.

"Do I do things that bother others, too, and I don't realize it?" she asked once. My daughter and I ponder, "Do we do things that bother others and we can't see ourselves clearly?" We need to come to God humbly for cleansing and love for others.

We need to take a sober look at ourselves from God's perspective. God did not give anyone all the plusses and another all the minuses. We must accept we have deficiencies too. We have areas that need developing with God's help. We must recognize the good in others, and love them while they are developing too. It takes not thinking of ourselves more highly than we ought to think.

I heard something new this week. "Do you know you can see only about one-third of yourself?" Even with the greatest effort, I can't turn around and see the back of my head, my ears, between my shoulder blades, my forehead, or chin. Much the same, others see me better than I see myself.

So, Lord, I pray, whatever faults or shortcomings I claim to find in others, help me overlook them. Help me love. I know not, I see not myself as others see me. I am undone before you.

The Real Issue

Romans 14:16-19

"What do *you* think?" Sister Sue* asked. Her question put me on the spot, for I had been mentally defending Sister Marie's* opinion. Now I wasn't sure what I thought.

The issue was neither right nor wrong, and I could see both points of view. However, there *were* some attitudes I should have been working on. Instead of condemning Sister Sue, I should have gone to the Handbook for All Problems.

There is the admonition: "And let none of you imagine evil against his brother in your heart" (Zechariah 7:10). I had been guilty there.

"Be kindly affectioned one to another with [sisterly] love, in honour preferring one another" (Romans 12:10). I had really slipped on that one too.

"Finally [sisters] whatsoever things are true ... honest ... just ... pure ... lovely ... of good report: think on these things" (Philippians 4:8). What a lot of valuable time I had wasted in wrong thinking.

After all, the kingdom of God is not a matter of painting the guest bedroom or leaving bare walls. Neither is it the proper way to landscape the mission property. "For the kingdom of God is not meat and drink; but righteousness, and peace, and joy in the Holy Ghost" (Romans 14:17).

"Let us therefore follow after the things which make for peace, and things wherewith one may edify another" (Romans 14:19). There is so much good work to do, that there is just not room for ill will or wrong thoughts.

Thank You, God. Your Book always has the answers we need. Give me grace to live it.

Tiger

Philemon

A favorite storybook in our home is *Tiger in the Teapot* by Betty Yudin. This simple child's story tells about a family who owned "a most tremendous teapot." One day when they wanted to make tea, it was occupied by a tiger! Each family member tried a different method for getting the tiger out.

Mama said, "Get out right away. I have to make tea."

Great Aunt reminded him of the courtesy of his ancestors.

Susie appealed to his common sense.

Some used threats of physical harm, Papa's anger, or calling the police.

One suggested the tiger get out for awhile, and then he could get back in.

But the tiger sat, quietly stubborn.

At last little sister arrived. She went up to the tiger and patted him on his head. She asked him if he was comfortable, if he was sure he wasn't cramping his long, lovely tail. She assured him he was welcome to stay as long as he liked, but wouldn't he rather come out and have tea with them?

And the tiger came out.

I think of this story when I need to help my teenager see the importance of obedience, or when a sister new in the faith makes no move to obey a Scriptural principle. Commands, appeals to common sense, or threats usually fail. A true concern for my fellow pilgrims' well-being and comfort and an invitation to something much better often brings about sweet cooperation.

It should. It was Jesus' method.

Broken Teapots

Proverbs 17:17-20; 18:24

I love old teapots—
Old teapots that have poured
many a cup of tea.
Fragile, but beautiful,
dainty rosebuds, tiny green leaves,
all sizes, shapes, and patterns.
Sometimes a teapot breaks,
and we glue it back together,
but it's never quite the same again.

Friendship is like a teapot—
Beautiful, but fragile,
it needs to be handled with care.
Precious moments shared
by two people
are special!
But, when that friendship
is broken, like a teapot,
it can be glued.
But it will never be quite
the same again.

Only God can take broken pieces—
and glue them
in such a way
that the cracks
don't show!
A friendship is restored!

My Speech

James 3

The Lord has been convicting me
    About the words I speak.
The nasty words I camouflage
    About someone who's weak,
Explaining in minute detail
    So everyone will know
The glaring faults another has.
    "How could she stoop so low?"

Perhaps the thing I heard is true,
    But is it very kind
To pass along each thing I hear
    Or comes into my mind?
Or do I stretch the truth a bit
    And use sarcasm cruel,
Explaining what my sister's like?
    Use I the golden rule?

If she should hear the words I said,
    I'd cringe and blush with shame,
Could I somehow those words collect
    I would, and take the blame.
I'd care if she would talk of me
    As I have done of her.
Why then should I be critical,
    And make her way unsure?

I want to learn to think before
    I speak my mind at all,
Lest in my thoughtless, careless ways
    I cause someone to fall.
For Christ has said, If I offend
    A little one in Him.
I'm better off not living here,
    Than cause eternal harm.

Lord, cleanse my mouth of wicked speech.
    Away with unkind words.
Erase the thoughtlessness I have.
    Choose carefully my words.
Please help me to be kind and true
    In everything I say,
By practicing the golden rule
    In speaking—every day.

A Secret

1 Timothy 5:10-13

*O*ur four-year-old grandson
    spent a day with us
    just a few days before Christmas.
He looked up at me,
    big brown eyes
    shining in happy anticipation.
"Guess what, Grandma,
    my mommy is making
    a dress for you for Christmas.
And it's a SECRET!"
    It was our special secret.
    What fun to watch his big
        brown eyes shine
    as I opened the package,
    and found the dress;
        our secret shared.
    Each time I wear the dress
    I remember the kindness of our
    daughter-in-law
        in sewing the dress,
    and the special secret
        shared with a little grandson!
Secrets shared are fun.
    But when someone unwisely shares
    a confidence, a need,
    a problem, or a burden
        on his heart, what

havoc, oh, what damage can be
done, when the secret is passed on.
"I really should not tell you this,
    just don't pass it on,
        but Mrs. Jones is having problems;
    we really should pray for her."
And so the gossip has begun,
    and it flies
    as if on wings, and someone
    is deeply pained
    and his reputation spoiled.
Dear God, enable us
    to see the harm of breaking
    a confidence
    entrusted to us,
    to share with You, alone!

I Made a Mess of Things

Psalm 51:1-12

I offended someone this morning. With a few thoughtless words, I made an awful mess of things. Why can't I learn to keep my mouth shut?

My heart is heavy; I feel so awful. I asked and received forgiveness from the offended person and from God. But I know I caused damage that hasn't been repaired. Plunged in remorse, I continue to berate myself.

My thoughts turn to King David. He committed a terrible sin. Penitent, he cried out to God for restoration and cleansing. God forgave him, but David had to reap the consequences.

I, too, have received forgiveness. I am doing what I can to make amends. Now I must forgive myself, as God has forgiven me.

"Restore unto me the joy of thy salvation; and uphold me with thy free spirit" (Psalm 51:12).

Faithful Are the Wounds of a Friend

Proverbs 15:32, 33; 27: 6, 9, 17

A sister from the church wanted to come over and talk. "Fine," I said, but I thought, *Why on a Monday forenoon?*

Soon I knew. "Is all as it should be between us? How is our relationship?" she asked.

It was the question I had feared from the moment she called. "Pretty good; mostly okay," I faltered.

She explained her growing concern that something was wrong. She sensed a discomfort when we met.

I didn't know what to say. I knew I didn't enjoy her friendship as I used to. A year ago or so I had felt inferior to her; maybe even intimidated by her. But now? I had hoped I had worked through that and buried it—had forgiven the offense. But suddenly it loomed as *the* barrier between us.

She made it easy to unload. She was ready to listen to my complaint. She took it humbly, evaluating it thoughtfully. She bore the offenses I had loaded on her through the space of a year. We shared freely, confessed our own sins, and parted refreshed and closer to each other and God.

"Lord, I'm so glad she came. My heart was dirtier than I thought. I believe the offense was really only imagined.

Thank You for the depth of her friendship— a friendship willing to bear reproach to restore our Christian love."

"Faithful are the wounds of a friend."

Be of One Mind!

Philippians 4:1-9

I beseech [beg] Euodias and beseech Syntyche, that they be of the same mind in the Lord" (Phil. 4:2). The two ladies—Euodias and Syntyche—are mentioned only once in the Bible. And why are they mentioned? Because they weren't getting along with each other. History tells us they were prominent women, possibly deaconesses. But the contention was so sharp between them that it nearly caused a church split!

We can only imagine what they disagreed about. Did it begin with jealousy or pride? Did it include self-righteousness and tale bearing? Perhaps it started with a small, unimportant thing such as who would have the privilege of hosting the church service. Whatever the cause, Paul's appeal was, "Rejoice in the Lord. Be moderate. Don't worry. Be thankful. Go to God for your needs." In verse 7, he promised them the peace of God if they would do these things.

How many of us need to be admonished in the same way? We may look at another sister and think, "Why does she have so many friends?" or "Why doesn't she have problems with her teenagers?" We may be constantly rubbing shoulders with one who seems to think her opinions matter most, and we would like a little recognition too.

If we harbor these envious "it's-got-to-be-my-way," thoughts, they will turn to pride and self-righteousness. The end result will be a huge wall of imagination blocking communication. But slanderous, cruel, and sarcastic remarks are heard, building an even higher wall.

But if we rejoice in the Lord and have a thankful heart, the wall will begin to crumble. As we fill our minds with truth and honesty, justice and purity, and lovely things of good report, we will become virtuous and full of praise. And the wall will disintegrate.

If my life were recorded for history, would it include admonishment to get along with my spiritual sisters? Would yours?

Saved by Grace

Titus 3:3-8

I grew up on a dairy farm, and there was always more than enough to do. Productivity is essential for survival on a farm. That concept was drilled into me early. While industriousness saved me from a lot of foolishness, there is another side to the coin. I developed a strong sense that my worth as a person was based on how well I performed. That idea has given me a lot of heartache.

The older ladies in our church's monthly sewing circle did a lot to help me out of this mental rut. In my younger years, they welcomed me and my small tribe with open arms. In spite of my limited sewing talents, I would work valiantly. But I was often interrupted by a runny nose, a wet diaper, or a shy child who needed comforting. It was frustrating until I began to realize that my older friends did not mind at all. In fact, most of these grandmothers took a genuine interest in the children and enjoyed having them around.

They would gently chide me, pointing out there is more to life than getting a lot done. They also reminded me the fellowship was important. I shouldn't worry if little was accomplished.

Time has moved on, and my children are no longer diaper babies. My arrival at the sewing is more dignified than it used to be, and there is more to show for it at the end of the day. I thank God who used my older friends to remind me that Jesus loves me, not because of what I do, but because of who I am in Christ.

The Older Women in My Life

1 Thessalonians 2:7-12

I consider myself neither the young nor the aged woman of Titus 2:3, 4. But now that I am past 40, I suppose I am in transition. However, this Scripture applies to me as well, since there are always women younger than I to influence. It is an honor to teach younger women.

The older women in my life have taught me so much. My mother, mother-in-law, grandmothers, and older women in the church have been wonderful examples to me. Most of what I am, I have learned from older women.

As I am passing through this transition from younger to older, I have developed some goals for teaching younger women. I would like to share them with you:

1. Let me encourage the young mother struggling with child discipline. Many times older women encouraged me to be consistent, to "hang in there." The results are worth it.

2. Let me encourage the young wife struggling with submission and obedience to her husband. As older women shared personally of their struggles in this area, I want to share how submission was the key to experiencing deeper love in our marriage.

3. Let me encourage the young wife and mother to be a "keeper at home." As I saw older women

managing their homes and making them safe
havens for their families, I followed their example.
I love being at home!

And finally, a word of encouragement to older sisters: be available to teach. Whether by example, a women's Sunday school class, or a word of encouragement, just be there! You will pass down much wisdom to the women of future generations. God bless you!

CHAPTER FIVE

"After This Manner . . . The Holy Women . . . Adorned Themselves"

1 Peter 3:5

Sarah

1 Peter 3:1-7

*S*arah, I need to talk woman-to-woman, heart-to-heart. Peter says I may be your daughter. You had none of your own, only a daughter-in-law, Rebekah. My name is Rebecca.

I admit there was a time I shrank from being your daughter. Obeying my husband, not afraid with any amazement, was too much for me. Fear gave me a distorted picture.

Now I'm learning that fearful, blind obedience is not very loving, especially if it brings down disaster on my "Abraham" or our marriage. Did you, with your beautiful, quiet spirit, appeal to Abraham to reconsider when he told you to say, "I am his sister"? (Genesis 12).

Still, he went ahead with his plan, so you obeyed, trusting God to protect you where your husband didn't. Sure enough, Pharaoh took you. Dear mother, weren't you terrified? Did you have icy feet? Did your stomach knot up as you waited on God to rescue you? Your confession would reassure me that being your daughter is within reach. Trusting God is a commitment even though one doesn't *feel* brave. But isn't God kind for sending peace after the cold-feet commitment is made?

Then when God did work a miracle and reunite you with your dear Abraham, how did you forgive him for his outrageous deed? He had asked you to half lie, to save *his* skin—as if yours didn't count. I know you did forgive. Your spirit could not have stayed quiet and fearless without forgiving.

Sarah, my husband is not a patriarch. But neither have

his failures been the magnitude of Abraham's. I used to think if God expected me to obey a husband, He owed me a flawless one. Anything less was too risky. But now, I will move over and give my man room to fail, to have weak areas all his life, to be human. It will give God space to work His divine design in our marriage. My feet may sometimes feel icy cold. But I will trust. Am I your daughter, Sarah?

A Mother-in-Law

Ruth 1:8-17

*I*ntreat me not to leave thee, or to return from following after thee: for . . . where thou lodgest I will lodge: thy people shall be my people and thy God my God."

It sounds like a husband and wife commitment to each other, a beautiful wedding text. In reality it was a daughter-in-law's commitment to her mother-in-law.

Ruth was a young Moabitess, a widow who loved her Jewish mother-in-law, Naomi. After Naomi's two sons and her husband died, Naomi planned to return to her hometown of Bethlehem. Because she loved Naomi and Naomi's God, Ruth chose to accompany Naomi. Later she became the grandmother of King David, the family line of Jesus.

We have all heard mother-in-law jokes, even horror stories. God wants us to build relationships with them, the mothers of our husbands.

As mothers-in-law, we need to love and cherish our precious daughters-in-law, our grandchildren's mother and our son's lover. We, like Naomi, must respect our daughters-in-law. And, as Ruth, we must choose to love and accept our mother-in-law.

Modern Day Ruths

Philippians 1:6, 9-11

*G*odly traits from the life of Ruth of old are being lived out in my sisters in the Lord around me:

I see

a willingness to leave and cleave, to be faithful to her minister husband, and to accompany him on church-related duties.

I see

Sister Catarina, with her husband, who readily invites the church family into their home for yet another church dinner, just as Ruth untiringly gathered grain in the field day after day.

I see

the quality of unquestioning willingness to follow instructions in my sister, Nancy. Her desire is, indeed, to her husband.

I see

many widows in our church family, who, like Ruth, know the grief of losing a husband. They, too, have learned to trust in the God of Israel.

I see

my own godly mother and Sister Sofia portray unswerving devotion and loving care to their aging husbands, just as Ruth cared for her aged mother-in-law.

I see

youthful sisters among us who may never marry. Yet they quietly live out useful lives for God and their families. Though Ruth's prospects of another marriage seemed dim, yet she chose to serve Naomi and her God.

I see

all of thee, my sisters, and many more unmentioned, who are Gentiles. As a Moabitess, Ruth should not have been allowed in the "church." Neither should we Gentile outcasts be allowed in the Church, except for God's unfathomable mercy. We, like Ruth, have been given a place in the family of God.

Modern-day Ruths. What a challenge and blessing they are to me.

Abigail, the Peacemaker

1 Samuel 25:18-31

*C*ompared to Abigail's churlish, evil husband, mine is very gracious and kind. Yet sometimes I need the peacemaking she demonstrated in her meeting with David—skills she undoubtedly acquired through years of stressful living with a son of Belial.

Abigail hurried. She decided on a course of action and did not allow fears or doubts to delay her.

There are some significant words that describe Abigail when she came to David: hasted, lighted, fell, bowed, and fell again. Her actions betray her humble attitude toward herself and her honor of David, the angry, insulted one.

Her words matched her actions, the first ones being, "Upon me." She was willing to take the blame and suffer the consequences, though she assured David she had been unaware of how Nabal had rejected David's messengers.

She spoke honorably of David, acknowledging he was on the Lord's side, that the Lord was protecting him and would do for David as He had promised.

Last of all, she appealed to his dignity and common sense. "Don't do anything you'll be sorry for later, or which will hinder God's blessing on your life."

When I have opportunity to make peace, I worry. What if my efforts aren't accepted? What if I make things worse? I certainly don't want to take any blame or criticism myself. And how can I honor and respect someone with wrong attitudes?

How much more effective would God's work of peacemaking be through me if I, like Abigail, would act promptly and wisely, humble myself, honor even one in the wrong, and kindly appeal to the offended one that he consider the present in light of the future?

The Bottom of the Barrel

1 Kings 17:8-16

*T*he dust swirled down the street in Zarephath as the widow left her house. There was not a green, growing thing in sight. The awful drought continued. No rains came. Though she rationed her supplies frugally, she and her son stayed hungry, and her resources continued to dwindle. Now, there was just enough meal in the barrel and oil in the cruse to fix cakes for one last meal. She headed toward the city gate to gather sticks for firewood.

A stranger stopped her. "Could you fetch some water for me?" he asked. As she started off to fill his request, he called after her, "And could I have a bit of bread too?"

She answered quickly, "All I have is a handful of meal and a bit of oil. I was going to make one last meal for my son and myself. Then we'll starve."

"Don't be afraid," Elijah told her. "Go, do as I asked. Then make some food for yourself and your son. The Lord God says the meal and oil will not run out till the rains come again."

With quickened steps and a joyful heart, she hurried to prepare the food. Think of it! The very day she reached the bottom of the barrel, God sent Elijah to her, and he asked her to share her last meal. Following this, God provided, not a full barrel of meal or a full cruse of oil, but the promise that her meager amount would not fail. She saw the bottom of the barrel every day, but she trusted God's promise. How thrilling!

We shrink at the testing of our faith in God's promises,

but to be of any worth, it has to be tested. At times we see the bottom of the barrel in our physical needs, at other times in our emotional or spiritual needs. Whatever the need, His promise is always sure. "My God shall supply all your need."

Blameless Elisabeth

Luke 1:5-25

I admire Elisabeth, the mother of John the Baptist. The Bible says she and her husband Zacharias, "were both righteous before God, walking in all the commandments and ordinances of the Lord blameless."

They were *blameless* in God's eyes! What a challenge! A dictionary definition of *blameless* is "innocent and guiltless." "Walking in all the commandments and ordinances of the Lord" speaks of obedience and faithfulness.

The Scriptures don't give a lot of details about this couple, but we do know Elisabeth didn't have an easy life. She endured the stigma of childlessness in a family oriented culture. Elisabeth faced this without yielding to the trap of self-pity, despair, and bitterness. This godly woman made a lasting impact on the world through her son John.

We have the same God Elisabeth and Zacharias had. Because God is our helper, we need not be discouraged or dismayed about our tendencies to fail. The Bible says He has given us everything we need to live godly in Christ Jesus. Praise His Name!

The Handmaid of the Lord

Luke 1:26-38

God spoke to a young woman
through an angel
Words of commendation.
"Thou art highly favored;
blessed art thou among women."
"Thou hast found favor with God."
Beautiful words, "favor with God."
Along with God's favor comes responsibility,
pain, sorrow, misunderstanding.
Mary, who was unmarried and
never had relations with a man,
was to become a mother.
A mother to the Son of God,
impossible with man,
possible with God.
Mary accepted God's plan for her,
"Behold the handmaid of the Lord;
be it unto me according to thy word."
I, too, am chosen of God.
His plan for me may include
pain, disappointment, and grief.

But I submit to His will
and, as Mary, I, too, will say
"Behold the handmaid of the Lord;
be it unto me according to thy Word."

Keep On Keeping On

Psalm 92:12-15

*A*nna, the aged prophetess, lived in the temple. She was available to those who wanted to consult with her. Am I available when people need me?

Anna was patient. She may have waited a lifetime to see the Messiah. It's worth the wait to see God's promises fulfilled. When God makes me wait, I want to remember Anna.

Anna persevered. Perseverance is not the same as waiting; it's strong, active, effective waiting. Anna kept on keeping on. She waited actively: fasting, serving God, sharing His message. When I get weary, I want to follow Anna's example of perseverance.

Anna was grateful. She gave thanks to the Lord after He so graciously allowed her to see the Messiah. I want to follow her example and thank God for the blessings He gives me.

Anna testified. After receiving what she wanted, she remembered others. She saw the Christ Child, then spoke to people about Him. May I faithfully testify to others about Him, too, as Anna did.

Anna served God in her old age. Her example shows me that no matter how old I am, I'm always the perfect age to serve the Lord. Like the aged prophetess, I want to keep on keeping on.

Anna

Luke 2:36-40

 nna! No Mara[1] you, though well you could be. Beautiful[2] maid from the land of happiness[3], deprived of your husband so soon.

Much is told of your bittersweet life in few words:
"Departed not from the temple . . .
"Served God day and night . . .
"Gave thanks . . .
"Spake of Him . . ."

You gently reinforce the teachings:
"Abide in Me."
"Pray without ceasing."
"Offer the sacrifice of praise."
"Teach all nations."

Anna, gracious lady, teach me.

1. Ruth 1:20: *Mara* means "bitter."
2. The women of Asher were known for their beauty.
3. *Asher* means "happy."

The Diseased Woman

Mark 5:25-34

*W*hat a sad condition! Considered unclean, this woman was an outcast, untouchable. According to the Law, anyone who came in direct contact with her had to bathe and change clothes. Besides, they had to refrain from participating in social functions for the rest of that day. Anything the woman touched—the chair she sat on, her bed, and anyone who touched her chair or bed—became unclean.

She couldn't visit her neighbors or friends without defiling their homes. She couldn't attend weddings. She couldn't even go to the temple.

Daily, she experienced the shame of feeling dirty and unacceptable. People despised and avoided her. What a lonely life!

She may have feared she would die. Who wouldn't think about dying after 12 years with her problem? On the other hand, she might have longed for death after living in such misery for so long.

Pale and weak from loss of blood, she probably lacked the energy to search for a cure. What was the use? She had suffered many things from many doctors and had only gotten worse. Besides, she had spent all her money.

It would have been easier to stay at home. It would have felt safer. She didn't relish accidentally touching someone and angering people by making them unclean. But when Jesus arrived in her community, she took the risk. Pressing through the crowd, she touched the hem of Jesus' robe.

Wonder of wonders! His power healed her immediately and completely.

She tried to hide, expecting condemnation. But Jesus didn't condemn her. He tenderly called her "Daughter."

Jesus changed her from a rejected woman to a daughter of God, from unclean to pure, from sick to well, from fearful and trembling to a courageous woman who testified in public.

Whatever their needs, He still changes women today.

Jesus Loved Martha

John 11:1-25

*J*esus loved Martha!" Those words bless me, for I am a Martha among Marys. I love to scratch off a whole "to do" list in one morning. I watch the clock and scramble to get lunch served *on time* to my family or big crowds. At sad partings, I am apt to be dry-eyed, analytical, and unemotional on the surface.

"Jesus loved Martha and her sister." At times I long to be a Mary. Marys take time to steal away and pray in the midst of busy morning work. They appear unpressured by the hands of a clock and take time to cuddle a child or encourage a sister. And lunch waits. Even mildly moving moments bring on tears and dabbing handkerchiefs.

Mary and Martha both went to meet Jesus. Both said, "If thou hadst been here, my brother had not died."

Martha's matter-of-fact statement was followed by two expressions of faith. These brought Jesus' words, which have comforted the grieving to this day, "I am the resurrection, and the life."

Mary's tearful, grief-laden words moved Jesus to tears, tears which soothe us today because Jesus, too, is touched by grief.

Martha or Mary, Jesus loves me. Mary or Martha, I can choose the good part of communicating with Him.

Priscilla

Acts 18:1-4, 24-28

*O*f all the women of the Bible, I admire Priscilla most.

The details are sketchy. But we do know she and her husband, Aquila, moved several times. Expelled from Rome, they lived in Corinth where Paul found them. Later, they moved with him to Ephesus. They must have returned to Rome, because Paul greeted them in his letter to the Romans. Later, when Timothy was in Ephesus, Paul sent greetings to them there. All this tells me that, though she was transplanted repeatedly, Priscilla blossomed for the Lord.

Priscilla strikes me as an intelligent and knowledgeable woman. She helped her husband explain the way of the Lord to Apollos. Her friendship with the Apostle Paul suggests she had a keen and ready mind to understand the truth of the Word.

Priscilla had an open heart and an open home. I know she was hospitable because the church met in her home in both Rome and Ephesus. Most of us face the challenge of getting ourselves and our children ready for church on time. Can you imagine what it would be like to regularly prepare your home for services too?

Priscilla was industrious, working with Aquila in their home business of tent making. Her faithfulness and loyalty to her husband impress me. Does the Bible ever mention Aquila without Priscilla? What a team! Side by side, they lived, worked, and learned. Side by side, they traveled, expounded, and served.

We women can't always be physically at our husbands' sides. But we can try to keep side by side with them emotionally and spiritually. And like Priscilla, we can be co-laborers with our husbands in the work of the Lord.

A Legacy to Future Generations

2 Timothy 1:3-6

*G*randmother Lois was an important influence in the life of young Timothy. Paul wrote about Timothy's sincere faith, "which dwelt first in thy grandmother Lois" (2 Timothy 1:5). Lois, researchers find, became a believer in Christ when Paul's first missionary journey brought him to her hometown of Lystra. Though only briefly mentioned, the grandmother's Christian influence on several generations is remarkable.

How do we grandmothers pass on a spiritual legacy to our grandchildren? Deuteronomy 6:1-7 admonishes us to keep His commandments by teaching them diligently to our children throughout the day. Timothy knew the Scriptures because Grandmother Lois had taught her daughter Eunice, who in turn grounded her son in his Biblical heritage. What an example for us!

The spiritual legacy of my Grandmother Beachy has been passed on to me. The testimony of her life, her love for the Word, and her prayers of intercession for her children and grandchildren are treasures that can never be taken away.

Dear grandmother, pass on your faith and knowledge of the Scriptures to your grandchildren. Stand in the gap with your intercessory prayers and claim them for the Lord. Be like Grandmother Lois, who, nearly 2000 years ago, influenced her daughter and grandchild for the kingdom of God, a legacy to future generations.

CHAPTER SIX

"Cleanse Thou Me From Secret Faults"

Psalm 19:12

Cleanse Me From Secret Faults

Psalm 19:7-13

I hope no one sensed how I really felt inside last night at the nursing home. I'm afraid some of it showed. It's awful to feel frustrated at someone. The young man in charge was determined not to sing where the old lady had told us to. He had his own plans. I wished I could calmly go along with his decision, but I was upset that he didn't listen to her. Even his mother stood back and said to him, "We'll do what you say." Then finally, after further thought, he gave in. But I had work to do on my attitude.

Today I am still meditating on my fault. God brought me to Psalm 19.

I need these verses. "Cleanse me from secret faults," keeps me from presumptuous sins and boldly pushing my way forward. The words, "who can understand his error," tells me my faults are not always clear even to me. Even as we sang, I didn't want this frustration to have dominion over me. I wanted to be clean.

Lord, coming to Your Word, Your statutes, Your law, I have been warned and directed. I have stood with my head bowed, and you have purified me. I can again be upright and innocent from the great transgression. "Let my words, and my meditations be acceptable before Thee, O Lord, my strength and my redeemer."

Don't Pity Me!

Psalm 13

*A*n aunt of mine was getting acquainted with others at a church gathering. One lady asked her to point out her husband.

"I'm not married," my aunt replied.

"Oh, I'm sorry," the woman apologized.

"Sorry!" my aunt exclaimed. "I'm not sorry! Why should you be?"

I've chuckled more than once at her witty reply, but it has also challenged me. What wonderful freedom from self-pity! What contentment! What acceptance of her place in life!

Self-pity keeps you from growing and producing fruit for Christ. He has provided all you need for growth, but self-pity stunts your spiritual life.

Self-pity is also blinding. It obstructs your view of how truly blessed you are. You cannot see God working to perfect you and make you a vessel for His use and glory.

Focusing on self constricts, limiting you to orbit the sphere of self while needs all about you go unnoticed. It seeks and thrives on pity from others. Poor me!

Living for self is a miserable existence!

Thank God He delivers from a sinful self-life! His Word promises and gives real freedom. "The Son shall make you free!" When we choose Christ as our Saviour from sin and allow Him to be Master of our lives, we are truly set free. His Word is our law and joy, and self is our foe. Christ calls us to deny self. Yes, no more sickly pleasure from pity parties: "I've been wronged," "I've been hurt," "Life's not fair to me." He calls us to rejoice in Christ in our suffering: "He's using this for my good and His glory," "I'm learning to love and forgive," "I trust God. He knows what He's doing."

Pride and Purses

Proverbs 16:2, 3, 5, 17-19

*H*ave you ever noticed that life has a way of humbling a person?

Staying presentable is a challenge in Guatemala where we have two seasons: muddy and dusty. I try to keep my family and myself clean and neat when we leave home. After all, our appearance affects our testimony for Christ. But our appearance can become a matter of pride.

Once sitting primly in the doctor's office, I glanced down at my dress. Horrors! Where did that huge spot of mud come from? Now what would I do? There was no convenient way to hide it or wash it off. I was on pins and needles trying to keep the purse over the stain. *If only my purse were a bit bigger!* I thought.

After several babies and years of dragging a gigantic diaper bag with me everywhere I went, I wanted a change, a different look. I went shopping for a new purse, something small. I didn't mind being a mother; I just wanted a break. Sorting through the handbags, I found the perfect one, *my* purse. Small, sleek, and lovely, this one would make me feel and look like a lady. I bought it, almost unable to wait until I could load it with my wallet and other feminine articles. I arranged it in my mind on the way home.

Once at home, though, I felt foolish. My wallet did not fit into my purse! So much for my pride! I kept the purse but had to buy a change purse for it. Whenever I carried that handbag, I was reminded of my pride.

Procrastination—Serious?

Hebrews 3:7-15

One summer evening, my husband asked me to go with him to visit a neighbor who was very ill. I wanted to work in the garden in the cool of the day. I told him I would go on Sunday. Imagine my horror when only an hour later we heard the neighbor had died of a massive heart attack.

We went right over to console the family. As we stood in a circle around his body, waiting for the ambulance, I was plagued with regrets—all because of procrastination.

Procrastination can come in very simple forms causing little pain or inconvenience. Sometimes it comes in larger doses resulting in greater harm or trouble to many people.

Our children must learn to be prompt. Procrastination can affect eternal destinies. It may start with carelessness about meals or chores. Later, it may include more important appointments, including worship services.

But the most important reason to be prompt is because of the great appointment we all must meet. Christ will come to receive His bride. The Bible says no man knows when it will be, therefore we must always be ready. We cannot plan to start getting ready this afternoon or tomorrow or on our next birthday, for it may be too late. Let us "Walk circumspectly . . . redeeming the time" (Ephesians 5:15, 16), for we don't know when we shall hear the final call for the most important appointment we shall ever have.

Mistakes

Philippians 3:12-16

*L*ast week I had a full day baking and preparing for company. I feel energetic and thought I'd dry some apples too. But that took longer than I expected. Bedtime passed. The kitchen was a mess, and there was still a bowl of sliced apples I couldn't let spoil overnight. My husband's patience was sorely tried. You know how that feels.

This week, I also had an overwhelming day. My children were sick, requiring almost constant care. Even though Regina baked my bread and Debra asked others to take my turn cleaning the church, an unexplainable tension was tightening my neck. When my husband came home from work, I realized where my tension came from. I was afraid all day of making the same mistake I had made the week before—of starting one job too many, one that would need to be finished up late. Of course, I was afraid of the same sad consequences.

Getting tense about it got me into worse trouble than the mistake would have. When my husband sized up my emotional exhaustion, he suggested I go for a walk while he looked after the children. After a long stroll with God through the back meadow, my fears calmed. The message that quieted my heart was not what I had expected. "Ye have need of patience with yourself. Trust Me for your own growth and your husband's. My work is not yet complete in either of you."

True, mistakes are for my learning. But to think that God can use them to bring good to others where I messed up is an overwhelming marvel of God's grace. Why waste such enormous emotional energy trying to protect myself from making mistakes?

Here, Father. I give You that fear and my self-protecting habits. YOU are my defender, keeping me from making mistakes that would harm, and using the mistakes I do make, for Your glorious purpose. I am excited to watch what beauty You will create out of my tangles.

Whose Servant?

Matthew 6:24-34

*P*ressed upon by many duties,
Pulled apart by more demands,
Hustling to complete one service,
Hurrying through each job's commands ...

Swiftly sewing shirts and dresses,
Madly mending rips and tears,
Cooking, stewing with the kettles,
Agitating clothes and fears ...

Children, not to love and cuddle,
But to help or hinder they;
House and dirt brought into order—
Tho' little ones may disobey.

"Wait a minute, Mama's darling,
Someone big is at the door—
Someone big to hear and counsel,
For a minute, hour, or more."

Visitation on the schedule,
Burdened souls to listen to,
Someone lost to bring to Jesus,
Then to counsel what to do.

Bible reading, must be given
Time. And where's the pow'r in prayer?

Weary head bows quick and whispers
Pleas for others in despair.

Prince of Peace observes her sadly,
She whose joy and gladness fled,
Clock's swift hands are lashing cruelly,
Guilt has come and left peace dead.

Then He catches her attention,
Offering to renew her peace.
"May I freedom find?" she asks Him,
"From this guilt obtain release?"

"Prince of Peace I gladly take thee,
Take Thy lightened burden now,
Acquitted from all condemnation,
In Thy service I will bow."

These Just-Getting-By Sundays

Psalm 100

I may as well face it; there are some Sundays I don't exactly enjoy. In fact, sometimes I almost dread them. Those are the Sundays we pack a lunch or take a chicken to eat with a church family and are gone all day, with morning and afternoon services. Being the nap-after-lunch type, I find a nap hard to do without. Sometimes I find myself just living for the homeward journey.

But what does God say about this half-hearted attitude toward His day? If I am fervent in spirit, can I be looking forward only to evening and returning home? In this frame of mind, am I giving thanks in everything? Am I rejoicing in the Lord always? Am I *pressing* toward the mark? Most importantly, am I giving unto the Lord the glory due unto His name in worship?

I have a responsibility to my brothers and sisters as well as my preacher husband and my children. What is my attitude saying to them?

I can be an encourager if I lift my thoughts to things above, not on how tired I feel, or how hot it is, or how boring this Kek'chi sermon seems.

Colossians 1:10 says, "That ye might walk worthy of the Lord unto all pleasing, being fruitful in every good work [surely going to church is a good work], and increasing in the knowledge of God [where better than in His house?]."

God gives an admonition with a promise in Matthew

6:33, "But seek ye first the kingdom of God, and his right-eousness; and all these things shall be added unto you." These things include sufficient bodily strength and the comforts of home that I miss.

Thank You, Lord, for opening my eyes through a fresh look into your Word. I choose to lay aside my own desires. Help me to find, instead, the blessings You wait to give those who honor You on Your day.

Holy Desperation

James 1:5-8

*L*ast evening I glanced through an encyclopedia one of the children left lying on the couch. My eyes "happened" to fall on the heading of "habits." *What would a secular writer have to say about this sticky subject?* I wondered. The author gave some basic concepts about habits and then gave some examples. He suggested that sometimes eating sweets is triggered by a feeling of loneliness. I was amazed that one of my major struggles was pinpointed by such an unlikely source. A wrong emotional focus connected to eating has been a problem as long as I can remember. I have tended to find security in food during my down moments. It's a deeply rooted habit. When my emotional tank is low, my thoughts just naturally turn to food.

The other morning the Lord and I had a long chat about this situation. I confessed my spiritual poverty to Him and followed with a strong commitment to the lordship of Christ in this area. I was desperate, and the Lord answered my plea. There was victory and a new freedom for several days. I wish I could say the struggle is over, but that is not the case. It seems the lordship of Christ must be renewed again and again in our problem areas. Maybe the underlying cause of my defeats is actually that I am short on desperation. Do I *really* want help? Am I *truly* broken on this point? "Lord, grant me freedom from this awful double-mindedness so that I may with sincerity choose *your* way."

God, be merciful to me a sinner!

Things

Colossians 3:1-4

I succumbed!
     I went to garage sales and auctions and bought lots of things. I packed up 39 boxes of things to bring home with me to Belize, besides some small buckets.

Now I am home again and wondering why I did that! Most of the things I didn't need. I had only one small notebook sheet of "needs." Where am I going to put these things? Who will buy the extra? And when am I going to have the time to take care of it all?

When I look back over furlough time, I am dissatisfied. I had hoped to spend large blocks of time alone with the Lord, time to write and read, time to be enriched. But I was subtly sucked into the snare of sales.

Now I cry, "O God, deliver me. Help me choose the heavenly, rather than the earthly." So praying, I view my possessions critically. I throw out what's unusable by me or anyone else. I remove more than I replace as I bring in kitchen things and new books. I don't want to spend so much time caring for and cleaning earthly things that I have no time to care for the heart needs of my family and friends.

My Last Two Mites

Mark 12:41-44

That Saturday morning I had counted out my money—all I had. I had $5.93. The checking account held $30 for Sunday's offering with a couple dollars left over. My $5.93 bought one dozen eggs and one gallon of milk to carry us through the weekend. While collecting my groceries, I saw I had enough yet for two half-gallons of the cheapest ice cream. Maybe we could have Sunday evening company.

I had just needed to replace our van. The purchase, tags, and taxes had dreadfully drained our resources. But the Lord had supplied just *enough*.

Why then was I lying across my bed at 3 p.m. weeping? I was perplexed. I was hurting, maybe angry, and probably selfish.

It was "workday" at church. The men were hanging siding. The hot afternoon had reminded Dwight of the ice cream I bought that morning. He thought it would refresh the men to have a treat and had called for it. (David used to say, "Bring up something to eat in the afternoon." Since he is gone, I find it hard to go to the church on "workdays" and I *don't* take snacks.) Now, would I take my ice cream? I did.

While the men ate our ice cream, I sobbed. I felt like the widow casting in her last two mites . . . except I wasn't happy about it. I wondered why I had to part with my ice cream! Why couldn't some other mother—or wife—think to feed the men? Again I saw the widow, a child in her arm and another at her skirt, casting in "all she had." She knew her utter dependence was on God. I saw Abraham also, ready to slay his son at God's request. Scripture says, "... for now I know that thou fearest God, seeing thou hast not withheld thy son, thine only son from me." Behold, God, not man, had asked for my ice cream. He asked, "Will you depend on *Me* to provide for tomorrow?"

Earlier today I had thought I was, but again I say, "I *can* depend on You, Lord."

Eye Glasses and Babies' Hands

Matthew 19:16-22

I'm glad I didn't wear eyeglasses when my children were babies. Whenever I hold my two youngest grandchildren, they try to pull my bifocals right off my face. They also pull at my veiling. In fact, they stretch for anything within their reach.

Humans seem to be born with a grasping nature. Just moments after his birth, one of our boys grabbed the obstetrician's scissors. It is a normal response for a baby to close his little fingers around anything that touches his palm.

The tendency to grasp continues throughout life. Toddlers clutch their toys. Teenagers grab for the car keys. And adults? Well, we hang on to our purses and wallets.

The Bible tells about a rich young man who asked Jesus how he could have eternal life. Jesus said, "Sell your possessions, give the money to the poor, then come follow me." The young man sadly turned away from the Lord. He found it too difficult to relinquish his riches.

It isn't any easier today, is it? Unclenching my tight fists may be the most difficult thing I have to do. Yet what blessings I receive when I finally manage to relax my grip, open my fingers, and offer my possessions to the Lord and to others!

The Mouth Speaketh

Matthew 12:33-37

I did not get along with the landlord's wife. She tried hard to be helpful, but I resented it. I didn't enjoy being told what to do, when to do it, or how to do it. I could make my own choices. After all, I was an adult with a husband and small children! I resented her intrusion. Without realizing it, I harbored bitterness toward her. I was sure our strained relationship was all her fault.

One Sunday evening it was time to leave for church. I had the children ready, but Vernon still had not come in from the barn. Finally he called to say something had gone wrong during chores, and he'd be late. "Go ahead with the landlord and his wife. I'll come when I can," he instructed.

"I'd rather walk than go with them!" I lashed out. Just then I heard a click on the line. Oh, no! I had forgotten that for Vernon to call me from the barn, he had to call someone else first and have that person dial our number. When the phone stopped ringing, he knew I had answered. Then he'd pick up and talk to me. It was complicated and unhandy, but it worked. The big hitch: the third party was not obligated to hang up immediately. Guess who had just hung up! I still cringe when I think of it.

I had been caught. Vernon knew it, too, and told me so.

"I don't care," I fumed. "It serves them right for eavesdropping."

But I did care. Deeply. I was so ashamed that I did not even want to go to church that night. I decided to wait and go with Vernon, even if it meant we'd all be late.

Since then, the landlord's wife and I have made peace. I have acknowledged that my bitterness and resentment were wrong. The Bible is right . . . "out of the abundance of the heart the mouth speaketh."

Please Protect the Treasures!

2 Kings 20:12-19

I was being accused of gossiping, my husband told me. I wanted to deny it. I tried to explain that a long time friend had asked me a few questions about a situation we were facing in our brotherhood. She had heard only one side of the story.

"Is it wrong to tell the other side?" I asked.

I tried to patch up the trouble I had caused, making several phone calls and apologies. I determined to be more careful about passing on information to uninvolved people. I certainly didn't want to be a talebearer.

A couple weeks later, our Sunday school lesson was taken from 2 Kings 20. As I studied about King Hezekiah showing the Babylonian envoys the fine treasures of his house, the Spirit spoke to me about sharing the heart-felt concerns of our congregation with someone who had no part or reason for knowing. The light dawned! I realized the carnal nature loves to put self forward by criticizing others. By doing this, I had not only been gossiping, I had also been showing pride in my own opinion. God hates pride!

I fell on my face before God and begged Him to forgive me for the hurt I had caused by talking when I shouldn't have, to give me wisdom to know when to share what, and to give me the courage to gather up the careless words where it was possible, and apologize where it was not. I desire that truth and peace may not only reign in my day but also for generations to come (2 Kings 20:19).

Bitterness

Hebrews 12:12-17

I had asked the Lord to show me myself as He saw me. But I didn't expect to see this—an appalling root of bitterness. No, not just a root, but a stalk and branches that had sprung up, spread, and bore defiling fruit.

I had been treated unfairly by close family members. A young co-worker wouldn't accept my opinions, and another couldn't see my priorities and wouldn't help meet my obligations. A sister, saved through the ministry of my husband and me, became upset when I suggested our relationship was like that of the Apostle Paul to the early believers.

These should have been small things, easily forgiven, if, indeed, they even needed my forgiveness. But I watered the root by remembering, then rehearsing the hurts in my mind. What's more, I repeated them to others. When new hurts came along, I added them to the old ones, causing quite a growth. I had failed to follow peace with all women and to apply the grace of God to each encounter.

My only source of hope has been to cry aloud to God to dig and cut until the root is gone. "Lord, uproot bitterness and plant blessing. Teach me thankfulness instead of self-pity and complaining."

The waters of Meribah *were* bitter. They were not improved by the grumbling of God's people. The only thing that sweetened the water was the placing of a tree into the water.

I, too, choose to place the tree, the cross, into my bitter

waters. The cross means dying to my complaints, my fault-finding, my pride, and my willfulness. It means saying, "Not as I will, but as Thou wilt" in every hurtful encounter.

Now I can live free of bitterness in a land of sweetness.

The Gossip Trail

1 Peter 3:8-14

*D*id you notice Mary went straight to the car after church last evening?" I said to Jane. "I wondered during the sermon how she would respond. Brother Paul was obviously speaking to her."

Jane said to Martha, "Mary was extremely upset over the sermon Sunday evening. Her toes were stepped on pretty hard. She couldn't hide the contempt on her face."

Martha said to Mildred, "Mary will probably decide our fellowship is not what she wants after all. She can't even accept the preaching of the Word without stomping out in a huff!"

Mildred said to Alta, "Did you hear that Mary is leaving the church? She doesn't think the preaching is sound, but it's really just what she needs."

Mary's mother said to Alta, "Mary had a severe headache Sunday evening. She went to her car immediately after the service. Later, she said how much she would miss the church fellowship if the privilege were taken away."

Alta stopped by our place for eggs Tuesday afternoon. Before leaving, she said, "Someone told me Mary is about to leave the church because she doesn't like the preaching, but Mary's mother said Mary would miss our fellowship if she wasn't able to come. Which do you think is true?"

Alta was gone before I could think clearly enough to respond. My knees felt weak, and my heart ached. Going to my room, I knelt by my bed. "Forgive me, Lord, and please help me straighten this out with Mary and whoever else may have heard the ripples of my horrid imagination. The next time I listen to a message, may I allow the Spirit to speak to me."

Fear Brings a Snare

Psalm 71:1-8

*W*ith Christmas coming, I sat down to send calendar cards to friends. The first one was for my dear friend Gladys. At the bottom I wrote Psalm 71:1, "In Thee, O Lord, do I put my trust: let me never be put to confusion." I read over the verse again. *That's a queer verse to put with these cards,* I thought. I didn't put it on the next ones. Two hours later that verse came to me with force and calmed a tempest within me.

Sunday we had come home from church and found a set of car keys lying near our front door. Who had been here during church, and how did they happen to leave without their keys? Nothing was familiar about them, not even the kind of car. I was apprehensive. Living without a husband leaves me with feelings I never had before.

My boys took the keys to the radio station as they went to work Monday morning, not wanting to leave them with me. I still felt uneasy about those keys. After the children went to school, I called my twin Martha and told her about them. We visited and hung up. Almost immediately she called back. She didn't want to scare me, but felt I needed to know what happened to her on Friday.

While shopping, she noticed a man watching her. It made her uneasy and she moved away. Finally he approached Martha and spoke. He told her he needed a wife, and he knew she had a sister who was a widow. Besides, he knew where I lived. Martha had hoped she wouldn't need to tell me this, but when I told her about the keys, she knew she had to.

I was shaken! I fell on my knees and wept to my God. Oh, the security a husband brings to his wife. Fear arose and took control. I pulled curtains and locked my doors. I would stay hidden in my house. Then my morning Scripture came to me. "In Thee, O Lord, do I put my trust: let me never be put to confusion." I bowed again before my God. I laid my bleeding heart in His hands and found consolation and rest. I opened a few curtains and relaxed in Him.

The Cheater

Psalm 103:8-14

This morning a man who once cheated my husband in a business deal came with a surprising request. He asked Eli to recommend him to feed-store owners so they would sell him chicken feed on credit. Eli explained that he couldn't because the man hadn't been honest with him.

When I heard about it, I exclaimed, "Why, that's ridiculous! What makes him think you would recommend him after he was so dishonest? He cheated you, and now he comes asking favors!"

But am I any better? Don't I sometimes cheat God, and then ask Him for favors? I'll admit it. I have.

God created me to glorify Him. I cheat Him when I fail to fulfill the purpose for which I was made.

God wants fellowship with me. I cheat Him when I neglect my quiet time with Him, then hustle and bustle through the day without talking to Him.

I cheat Him when I squander the precious time He gives me in worthless conversation or in doing nothing.

When I spend God's money on things I don't need, I know that cheats Him too.

Dear God, You have showed me I am no better than the man who came this morning. Thank You for granting me favors I don't deserve. Help me not to cheat You anymore.

Amen

Proverbs 11:24-31

I caught myself singing softly, "Yes, my heart says 'amen' to Thy will, Lord, and I know that thou lovest me still."

When I sang that song as a youth, I thought of going to faraway places or making great sacrifices. Tonight it merely meant giving one more man a bed and breakfast so that he could visit his sick daughter in the hospital tomorrow.

That's such a small thing to say "Amen" to. But the memory of an earlier night lingered with me. A couple taking their nine-month-old son to a doctor in the capital needed a place to stay for a day and a night. The very young mother was helpful; she swept the floor and washed the dishes. She also helped herself to cake, stored in a covered container. She used the fans, toys, and books. The hardest to bear was when she and her husband helped themselves to noisy showers and bright lights at 3:00 in the morning so that they could catch the 4:30 bus.

But what condemned my heart was two nights later when they again needed lodging on their way home. I was still irked by their thoughtlessness. I gave them bedding, but asked them to sleep on the veranda rather than in the living room.

The Lord sharply rebuked me for my action. I repented and attempted to make the rest of their stay pleasant.

I want the Lord's blessing and His love to reach through me, so I say, "Amen, and I know you love me."

Pickup Doors and Swords

Psalm 27

*E*very time I open the pickup door on the passenger side, I have to give the handle an extra hard jerk. And every time, irritation threatens.

You see, a novice was once "proving" to my husband that he knew how to drive when he crashed right into a cahune tree. "My" door got smashed. They tried to fix it and smooth out the dents, but it will never be the same again.

I am a Christian. There must be something better than this continual animosity I feel. I'm tired of being upset. Besides, doctors tell us it's not even healthy. Most importantly, giving way to anger is sin in God's sight.

Now I know! Having a *sword* in hand every time I work that door will help bring victory!

Psalm 27:1 fits into my hand first: "The Lord is my light and my salvation; whom shall I fear? the Lord is the *strength* of my life; of whom shall I be afraid?"

Oh, but verse 2 really strikes the spot: "When the wicked [one and his demons], even mine enemies and my foes, came upon me [as I struggled with that stubborn door] to eat up my flesh [and consume me with displeasure], they stumbled and fell [because I met them with a sword]."

Verse 4 speaks my desire. It describes something better, more satisfying and healthy compared to self-destructive anger. "That I may dwell in the house of the LORD all the days of my life, to behold the beauty of the LORD, and to inquire in his temple."

If I *abide* in His presence, "For in the time of trouble

[when annoyance threatens at that inexperienced driver] he shall hide me in his pavilion: in the secret of his tabernacle shall he hide me; he shall set me up upon a rock." (Psalm 27:5).

"And now shall mine head be lifted up above mine enemies [of my soul] round about me: therefore will I offer in his tabernacle sacrifices of joy;" and instead of grumbling at the faulty door, "I will sing, yea, I will sing praises unto the LORD" (Psalm 27:6).

Pickup Doors and Forgiveness

Isaiah 38:17; Micah 7:18-20

It's me again, Lord, about that pickup door. I'm so glad for another secret You've shown me. Something I missed last time ... about forgiveness.

The hour was late as we returned from a trip to Belize City, 200 miles and seven hours away. Joyce had fallen asleep long before on the second seat. To keep ourselves awake, Daniel and I were listening to tapes we had borrowed from another mission along the way. One message was on forgiveness.

Though I have forgotten most of that sermon, a key thought stuck. It had to do with forgetting. Forgiveness also means forgetting. But too often we memorize instead. Any teacher knows the rule for memorization: repetition. Over and over again. Daily. Several times daily.

Blind me! That's what I had been doing with Juan.* Opening that pickup door often triggered memory work.

Forgiveness is a choice. Can it be that forgetting is also a choice, deliberately turning our minds to something profitable and good and staying our minds there.

Thank You, Lord. You knew how badly I needed this lesson on forgetting. And strangely enough, I can almost thank You now for allowing the smashed door in the first place. Otherwise I would have missed this valuable lesson.

I choose to forgive Juan, and I choose to forget.

*Name changed.

Boils

Isaiah 1:4-6, 16-20

*W*hen our oldest children were small, we took a two-week trip to Belize. We enjoyed visiting with friends but had trouble appreciating the heat and all the biting bugs.

Vernon, Susana, and Benji all returned to Guatemala with battle scars.

Susana had scratched her bites until she had pus-filled sores all over her. The infection seemed to be right under the scabs. The other two had fewer bites, but they were deeper. Some of them turned into boils.

A visit to the doctor was followed by a round of antibiotics. Vernon and Susana recovered rapidly. But two-year-old Benji, even after medication, continued to suffer from a festering boil on his back.

Finally, I decided to lance it. Sticking a needle down into the center, I was amazed at its depth. I squeezed gently, and the nasty stuff poured out. Then, I firmly applied more pressure, feeling very sympathetic for my howling son. Suddenly, with a pop, the core erupted. When the blood began to run pure, I felt sure I had gotten it all. I cleansed the sore and coated it with an antibiotic salve and rebandaged the wound.

The next day I could see a marked improvement. Within a few days the boil had completely healed.

Some thought I had been terribly cruel to inflict such pain on my young son, but I knew that to cure him, the infection had to come out. Our doctor assured me I did the right thing. He told us it would not have made any difference how much antibiotic Benji took, until that root was out, nothing would have helped.

I thought how it is with our spiritual lives. We can doctor and doctor, put on salves, and take all sorts of remedies. Until the root problem (sin) has been dealt with, we cannot, and will not, experience true healing. God has to squeeze the core of the boil out . . . even when it hurts!

CHAPTER SEVEN

"Being Filled With The Fruits of Righteousness"

Philippians 1:11

God's Woman

Romans 16:1, 2, 6, 12

God's woman . . .
    Is beautiful from the inside out.
    She has those inner qualities
        that never leave a doubt.
    She knows not only who she is,
        she knows to whom she belongs.
    Her identity is in Christ,
        she's made by His design
    A part of God's great master plan,
        a plan that is divine.

God's woman . . .
    Her ornament is from the heart,
        a meek and quiet spirit;
        hidden, inner beauty,
        of a woman of great price!
    The joy of living
        expressed to all who know her
        comes from a life of giving.
    Giving of herself, not only to her family,
        but to anyone in need,
        a touch of God's love
        by kindly word or deed!

God's woman . . .
 Is beautiful within,
  but the glow of that beauty
  shines on the outside,
  transforming ordinary women,
 using them in special places
  to share God's love to all!

Like a Palm Tree

Psalm 1

The palm tree is among the most beautiful plants God made. Graceful, slender, and tall, it makes a beautiful picture as its fronds wave in gentle breezes. However, the most striking feature of the palm tree is not its beauty, but its usefulness.

The fruit from palm trees is the daily food of millions. Its leaves and trunk provide timber and thatch for shelter. Fibers from palm leaf-stems are made into ropes and brooms. The sap of some palms can be made into food and drinks. Some people make buttons and carvings from the seeds. Other products and by-products of palms are baskets, mats, hats, wax, oil, and soap.

The Bible, in Psalm 92:12, promises that we can be like a palm tree. It says we can keep on bearing fruit—even in old age. The person who meditates in God's law and delights in it day and night will be "like a tree planted by the rivers of water, that bringeth forth his fruit in his season; his leaf also shall not wither; and whatsoever he doeth shall prosper" (Psalm 1:3).

Lord, let me be beautiful and productive like the palm tree.

My Kitchen Floor

1 Timothy 6:6-9

*W*hen we moved here more than ten years ago, the kitchen floor stood out like a sore thumb. Even the inconveniences of my Central American mission house had not conditioned me for this thorn in the flesh. The rough, abrasive linoleum impressed me as a worn-out specimen from a by-gone era. Even now, as I sit at my kitchen table, the impression remains. The once attractive, green surface is not any easier to keep clean than it was 11 years ago.

Times without number, I belly-ached for a change, but to no avail. It's not that my husband doesn't care. There is just too much month left at the end of the money.

Strangely enough, I'm at peace with my kitchen floor. While I do have occasional flare-ups, I generally don't see red flags when I look down. I think the verse that helped me most is 1 Timothy 6:8, "And having food and raiment let us be therewith content."

My attitude didn't change overnight; rather, it was a gradual process. As I reminded myself that we have plenty of food and clothes, I gained a different perspective. The secret is a focus on what I have, not on what I don't have.

That White Kitchen Floor

Ezekiel 36:24-28

A white kitchen floor! How beautiful and clean it was! At last, I had the floor for which I had longed. But what a silly longing for a farmhouse! Everyone entering our home has to walk through the kitchen. It didn't take me long to realize I had made a poor choice. Actually it was more than a poor choice; it was a very bad mistake.

Nevertheless, that white floor taught me a few things I needed to learn. First, it taught me that "things" do not make me happy. (I don't know how often I'll have to learn this.)

And often when I scrubbed it, I prayed that my life would be like that floor—every speck of dirt showing so I would want to be immediately cleansed, pure, and white.

Finally, there was a lesson on unconditional love. One day my son walked across the kitchen with muddy boots. "Cheryl," I said to his four-year-old daughter, "Look what your bad dad did."

She replied, "Grandma, he's not a bad dad. He is my precious daddy." How thankful I am to have a daughter-in-law who teaches her children that they have a precious daddy.

The white kitchen floor eventually wore out, and we replaced it with something more practical. But I want to remember the lessons it taught me.

I want to remember that joy comes from within and not from outward circumstances. It is my prayer that the generations following me will realize that beautiful kitchen floors are no comparison to inner peace.

Busy Hands / Quiet Heart

Isaiah 30:15-21

*M*y hands are busy these days,
>   very busy.
> There's always lots to do
>   with a family of eight.

All day long I can go
>   from one thing to the next—
>   organizing,
>   picking up,
>   managing,
>   moving right along.

Busy hands.
Yes, busy hands are a blessing
>   and a gift.
I was taught to work,
>   and I love to work.
But somehow I feel myself
>   being so much,
>   too much,
>   like Martha.
I have a busy SPIRIT;
>   and when I have a
>   busy spirit,
>   I don't have a quiet heart

to hear from Him
　　what is the next right thing to do.
And sometimes the next right thing
　　is to STOP
　　　　everything,
　　sit down
　　and read a book to my children,
　　　or play tag,
or go on a walk,
　　or listen to their talk.
Or sometimes the next right thing
　　is to sit at His feet
　　　and HEAR Him.

Lead me, O Father,
that I may
　be faithful daily
　　like Mary
　in choosing that good part
　　which shall not be taken away
　　　from me.

For We Know Not

James 4:13-17

*M*y to-do list for today is long—long and interesting. There is wash for my family, and an order of magnetic signs for a truck. I need to finish framing certificates and deliver them to my friend Teresa. I want to call Lucy to see how she is and remind her I'm praying. Thora is to come about their order of restaurant menus. I want to do something special for my daughter Emily since it's her birthday—maybe cupcakes for her students. The list goes on.

Washing is at the head of the list and can be going on while I work on other things. Then, as always, I wonder how many interruptions will crop up and demand my time.

I ask the Lord in my morning devotions to guide my day in His paths. Soon my two daughters come for help with their hair, and then breakfast preparations are underway. Emily leads in prayer at the table and asks the Lord to direct our day and help us keep our priorities right and honor Him. With that I feel myself relaxing.

I'm relaxing because I do not need to carry my tasks and push them through. I can rest in God. Most tasks can go with the flow of the day, and God can direct my priorities so His will is done. I know already that the mothers of Emily's students are bringing in pizza, cake, and ice cream for her birthday at lunch, and I am invited.

I relax again, willing to let the Lord lead. So "if the Lord will, we shall live, and do this or that."

In Focus

2 Corinthians 4:15-18

*Y*ears ago, my sister and I owned a little old-fashioned Brownie camera. It took good, sharp outside pictures. Later, I graduated to a pocket camera with a built-in flash. This was definitely a step up. No more double exposures. Inside pictures became possible. I was pleased.

After my husband and I were married, I got to use an even more advanced camera. His had adjustable focus and shutter speeds. Now I could even take inside pictures without a flash. I could take fascinating close-ups of beautiful flowers without blurring. What a pleasure!

I noticed when I focused on items close by, the background blurred. Likewise, when I focused on faraway objects, the closer ones blurred.

Now years later, the Lord has helped me understand a spiritual lesson about focus. When I feel overwhelmed with laundry day, it may be because of a wrong focus. I can choose to focus on the time laundry takes away from more important jobs. Or I can choose to think of God's blessings to me through my husband and our children. I can fuss about having to empty sawdust from my husband's pants pockets. Or I can focus on how thankful I am for his steady job, his good health, and his willingness to work hard for us. When helping my daughter with her homework takes precious minutes from my afternoon, I can get upset about it, or focus on the privilege of having a daughter, and that I am physically, mentally, and spiritually able to help her.

We can choose to focus on earthly things, or we can focus our "lens" on what is spiritual. Paul reminds us that earthly things are only temporal. Spiritual things are eternal. If I choose, by God's grace, to focus on what is spiritual, it will affect the quality of my attitudes toward God, others, and myself. It will produce within me the beautiful fruits of cheerfulness and gratitude. It will make my life a glory to my Lord.

Used by permission of Rose Mary Bontrager.

Pleasant Words

Proverbs 16:21-24

How often I have reminded my children
        of this verse—
            "Speak pleasant words.
            Have a sweet spirit."

And how often I have prayed
        for pleasant words and a
        sweet spirit
            to flow from me each day.

Just today it hit me—
        what puts sweetness in my spirit?
            and in my soul?
        Isn't it pleasant words?
        And what makes it easier
            to speak pleasant words?
        Isn't it having a sweet spirit?
How simple.
How uncluttered
        and freeing . . .
            and utterly challenging.
DAILY this mother needs
        divine influence
            to speak only pleasant words
                to my family
            so that sweetness will flow.

And DAILY I need
   divine influence
      to have a consistent sweet spirit
         so that pleasant words will come forth.

Acceptable to God

Proverbs 25:11-15

*L*et my words, my meditation,
    be acceptable to You, O my God.
    You are my strength
    and You are the One who redeems.
You are a Redeemer God.
    You can make a new heart in me from which come
    words of kindness, instead of anger;
    words of love, instead of criticism,
    joyful words, rather than hurtful.
My words should be as apples of gold
    in a beautiful frame of silver.
You are able to change my thoughts,
    to be acceptable to You, as
    I make a conscious effort to dwell on
    those things that are pure, honest, and just;
    not thoughts of gossip or low self-esteem,
    but only those You will accept.
    Thoughts that will
    make me to grow
    into a person in Your likeness.
You, O God are my strength,
    and You are the one who enables me
    to be a woman who fears you.

Commendation or Complaints?

Ephesians 4:29-32

*A*s we pulled up to the church in Santa Cruz this morning, we were greeted by a welcome, but uncommon, sight. Three little girls were lined up outside watching our arrival. As we climbed from the truck, we could see the rest of the minister's family coming down the trail. Too often, they've been late. My heart was glad and ready to worship as we gathered inside. Later I made it a point to commend them for being on time.

On the way to church, Julia had noticed the mirror on the driver's side had been replaced. "Be sure to thank the mechanics," I said.

Isn't it easy to complain about people and cracked mirrors? Try the commendation approach. Look for areas where it can be honestly done, and see if it doesn't make a difference—in them . . . and yourself.

The Apron of Servanthood

Philippians 2:3-8

*M*issionaries are so hospitable. On a recent trip to Central America, our family experienced hospitality in a new way. I tried to analyze what made it extra special. I saw that many wore the apron of servanthood.

Once we were enjoying supper and fellowship with a family. We filled our plates in the kitchen then went to the living room to eat. The hostess waited till last. When she came into the living room, every seat was taken.

"*This* is my favorite place to sit," she said graciously, as she sat on the floor. I saw the apron of servanthood tied around her waist.

In home after home, I noticed the aprons of servanthood worn by our missionary friends had threads of humility woven into their fabric. As they generously shared with us simple meals, medicine for our sick children, a bar of soap, and laundry facilities for our mounds of dirty clothes, the spirit of humility was evident. They sacrificed time from their busy schedules to take our family sightseeing or to our next destination. It was service with humility.

Lord, how many times have I served others without the apron of servanthood? And how many times have I served without humility? I picture You washing Your disciples' feet with a towel wrapped around Your waist. You, as the Messiah, the King of Kings and Lord of Lords, stooped to wash Your disciples' feet.

Humbly I wear the apron of servanthood.

Care-y

1 Chronicles 12:37-40

*A*nd there they were with David three days, eating and drinking: for their brethren had prepared for them" (1 Chronicles 12:39).

Recently I noticed a note my daughter wrote to a friend. I thought she had misspelled "Carey," but when I looked it up, I saw it was correct after all. Having a name with "care" is simpler than *being* a person who cares.

We have been entertaining visitors—sometimes more than one group at a time. I found myself focusing on *me* and wondering how much more I could handle. I felt, oh, so weary, and was finding meal planning and laundry a chore.

The verse from Chronicles rebuked me. David's visitors were entertained willingly and gladly. Everyone was happy: both the partakers and the preparers; and the feasting was *so* good that they stayed three days!

Could my name be "Care-y"? Do I care about my guests? Or would I just as soon they hadn't come? Am I concerned that *they* enjoy themselves?

O God, You who know the hearts of women, know that my heart hasn't always been perfect in this. Thank You for also knowing the discouragement that comes with physical weariness, and that You will not send more than I can handle. I cast myself, with all my limitations, on Thee. Make me a Care-y for Thy honor and glory. Amen.

How, Lord?

Hebrews 13:1-5

*D*o you ever find it difficult to give hospitality without grudging? I don't like to admit it either. One day I prayed, "How, Lord? Please show me how." Through His Word, God showed me these three steps.

1) **Do it as unto Me** (Matthew 25:40). Now I try to treat each guest as I would treat Jesus if He were to drop in for a meal.

2) **Imagine your guest as an angel** (Hebrews 13:2). That often brings a chuckle. "Well, if this is an angel, he's very well disguised!"

3) **In everything give thanks** (1 Thessalonians 5:18). Can you give thanks and grumble at the same time? It's even more difficult than patting your head with one hand and rubbing your tummy with the other. Giving thanks for an unexpected guest helps me give hospitality willingly and gladly.

Company Again?

Matthew 25:31-46

*M*om, look at this kitchen. We'll probably get company today," my daughter said one morning. The kitchen and dining room tables were both piled high and would remain so until we finished our painting project. *No*, I thought, *we can't have company today.*

But at 10:00 a.m. the phone rang. My daughter answered. "I'll let you talk to Mom," she said, handing me the phone.

The caller explained that two brethren needed a place for lunch. "Does it suit you?" he asked.

"No, not really," I replied. I tried to explain the situation, but he assured me the brethren wouldn't mind at all.

I glanced at the stove, which was the only empty surface in the entire dining room or kitchen. "Well, I suppose I could cook the dinner here and take it to Grandma's house next door to eat," I somehow managed to say.

"That will be fine," he agreed, "I'll send them right over."

Two hours later we were sitting around the table eating instant mashed potatoes and hamburger gravy. I thought about the kindred spirit we can have in Christ.

What did I teach my daughter about hospitality that day? I had a choice. I could either accept it and enjoy eating lunch with two strangers (and we did), or I could fuss and complain about how unhandy and awkward the situation was.

In as much as ye have done it unto one of the least of these my brethren, ye have done it unto me.

Baby Peter

Colossians 3:22-25

*T*ime: 12:30 a.m.
A cold drizzly rain.
An empty bottle.
A hungry baby swaddled in a towel.
My introduction to five-week-old Peter.

I boiled water and tried to stir up an adequate formula from the powdered milk we had on hand. When I picked him up, I smelled the smoke of Indian homes. While I fed Peter, his weary father rested on the sofa.

One night of caring for a baby isn't bad, I thought. *Tomorrow the father will take the child home with him since Peter can't stay with his sick mother in the hospital.*

But the mother had to be flown to a bigger hospital, and the father had to go along. Little Peter stayed with us.

Waking several times a night to perform the feeding ritual began to wear on me. I complained about the invasion of my sleep and the intrusion on my busy days.

Then in the third watch of the fourth night, a Scripture began repeating itself. "Whatsoever ye do, do it heartily, as to the Lord."

"Oh, to You, Lord? Yes, what a privilege to care for the Christ Child."

My shoulders still ached. My eyes still craved sleep. But my heart was free from the burden of complaint as I snuggled baby Peter closer.

Knowing Enhances Serving

John 13:1-17

*H*umble service requires heart knowledge. What Jesus knew enabled Him to humbly wash the disciples' feet. What He knew helps me.

Jesus knew His time. It was time to leave this world. I know my time. It's short. What service wouldn't I do for the Lord, if I knew today was my last day? Last day, last year, or last century, His work is urgent, and my time to do it is now.

Jesus knew His Commander-in-Chief and the responsibility He had been given. I know my Lord. I know my responsibility. My life is not my own to live as I please. My work is not the same as Christ's or that of any other earthly person. It is unique to me.

Jesus knew where He came from. He was the only begotten Son of the loving Father. I am created and bought by the same loving Father. My life has purpose and meaning because of my origin.

Jesus knew where He was going. Back Home! I, too, am going Home after my short stay here. There will be rewards for loving service. But what is the most blessed thing about Home? God is there.

Jesus knew His enemy. Judas was only Satan's tool. Knowing this, Jesus did not respond to Judas in anger, only deep sadness. Those who seek my hurt are allowing Satan to use them too. Knowing this enables me to respond as Christ did.

The Source of all knowledge and the perfect example of humility said, "If ye know these things, happy are ye if ye do them."

Lending

Luke 6:27-38

*A*s Brother Kenneth spoke from Luke 6 on lending, I remembered an experience David and I had years ago. I did not encourage him to lend, rather, I tried to discourage him. But David listened to this Scripture. It led him. It happened this way.

Two neighbor youths came to our door one Sunday afternoon and asked if they could borrow a spare tire from one of our vehicles. They were sure it would fit their car, which had a flat. I heard David say, "Sure, I'll get it for you."

When he stepped back inside to get his shoes, I told him I wasn't so sure about this. Those boys looked rough to me and poor risks for a loan. Years earlier their older brother and a couple others had broken into our house and ransacked it for plunder. I did not think David would get the tire back if he loaned it. I told him so.

"God says to lend not hoping to receive again," David said firmly. He was confident the tire would be returned when theirs was fixed.

Confident he was doing right, David didn't look at who they were. I stood back with awe and respect as he sent them off with his tire.

I know God's Word is to be obeyed. God is right, and He wants men to see godliness in shoe leather, that they might see Him. Verse 36 says, "Be ye therefore merciful, as your Father also is merciful."

Look No Further

1 Timothy 2:8-15

The other day we found ourselves creeping through nerve-racking, bumper-to-bumper traffic. To my surprise, Vernon slowed and let several cars pass us.

When I asked why, he told me he had dropped back on purpose. "I got tired of being beside that liquor truck with the nearly nude woman displayed on it." My heart warmed to realize anew that my husband was trying to keep his mind pure. It's so difficult these days.

Then I saw a huge billboard at a major intersection. There was no way to miss it, a woman clothed in only a skimpy bikini. The caption screamed, "LOOK NO FURTHER!" It was an advertisement for car parts. What a woman's body has to do with car parts is beyond me. I wondered how many men looked no further and looked again.

The way women's bodies are used for advertisements really upsets me. I want to cry out and tell the world what I think about the whole rotten mess. But what can one woman do with so pervasive a problem?

With God's help I can do my part. Do I dress provocatively, tempting men, or do I cover my body decently? Are my dresses long enough and loose enough to hide my figure? Do I comb my hair in a becoming way or leave it exposed to catch attention? Am I careful how I act?

We can encourage our husbands and sons in their determination to remain pure. And we must pray for them. Faithful women can make a difference.

A Quiet Heart

Proverbs 17:1-6

*T*hese days are busy days,
    full of activity
        and things to do
            and places to go—
        even for stay-at-home moms.

There are voices calling
        from here and there
        and everywhere—
      "Come help me"
        "Come hear me"
          "Come buy me."
All these "doing" things
    must not take my time and attention away
      from focusing on "being."

Yes, there are things I must do,
    places I must go,
      out of necessity in being a mother.
My family needs groceries
    and need clothing.
Yet in my children's
    formative, tender years
I must work on contentment,
    and ask for wisdom to use
      what I have in my hands,
      instead of reaching out for all the "extras."

I must make it a priority
    to focus on relationships
        with my family,
    for each member is a treasure
        to invest in for eternity.

I must make it a priority
    to give my children
        my time,
    for I am commanded to teach them diligently.

I must keep a quiet heart
    so that I can
        hear His voice
           to guide me.

I must focus on
    being . . .
        rather than doing.

Little Things

Matthew 10:38-42

ord,

Thank You for showing me
the importance of little things.
I think Your message
is finally getting through.

It began with the U.S. coins
village children brought
to be changed into
useable Belizean currency.

You know I was tempted
to be impatient.
"Why are they wasting
my valuable time? Calling
me to the door just to change
one "lee," twenty-five cents.

But You kept on testing me,
until one day I saw
that little coin as a
cup
    of
       cold
          water.

You were asking me to give
one just as graciously
as the other.

Now I know that You see
and will be pleased when I
give it in Your name
willingly,
    cheerfully,
        sweetly.

Thank You, Lord, for this
important lesson on
little things.
I almost missed it!

Grace Enough, Part 1

1 Corinthians 15:9, 10; 2 Corinthians 12:6-10

*L*ong ago my twin Martha told me one meaning of *grace* is "the ability to do things God's way." I liked that and have often applied it to verses I read.

"By the grace of God I am what I am," Paul wrote in 1 Corinthians 15:10. It is by my doing things God's way, by God's enabling, that I am what I am. The verse reads further, "His *grace* which was bestowed upon me was not in vain." Paul says the grace bestowed, or the resource appropriated for strength, was used, not wasted.

In 2 Corinthians 12:9, God says, "My grace is sufficient for thee: for my strength is made perfect in weakness." When I am too weak to choose the right, God can, by His strength applied to my life, make me able for the task or decision and give me courage. I am given the ability to do things God's way in my time of need.

The grace of God also protects us. Christians are promised that no temptation will come for which there is not strength to bear or a way to escape (1 Corinthians 10:13). God helps us stay on His holy way.

Grace, the ability to do things God's way!

Grace Enough, Part 2

Hebrews 4:1, 2, 14-16

One day last summer we went to Martha's garden and found all the corn down. A storm had passed through and *all* the corn was down in one tangled mess. Not a single stalk stood over a foot high. Martha had been expecting to pull corn for freezing any day. Her response was full of grace, and it blessed me. I wrote the following as a tribute to her.

Dear Sister Martha,
>   Yesterday—
> We found you in the cornfield
> Trying to take the yield
> From the stalks
>   that lay on the ground
>   all around.
>
> I saw in you
>   no frustration
>   no fuss, or fret,
> Just the sweetness
>   of the corn on the ground.
> With it—
> I sensed
>   that you had drunk the cup,
>   and with it GRACE was given.
> It was lovely for us who entered
>   your mangled cornfield.

Each "cup" given us
    is full of "grace,"
    (the ability to do things God's way.)
We can use the grace given
    or pour it on the ground,
    or only now and then take a sip—
Yesterday you took the cup
    and drank it,
    and you were filled with GRACE.

"Let us therefore come boldly to the throne of "grace" that we may obtain mercy, and find "grace" to help in time of need" (Hebrews 4:16).

I'm glad we could help you do your corn today.

"The grace of our Lord Jesus Christ be with you. Amen" (Romans 16:20).

A Grain of Mustard Seed

Matthew 17:14-21

A mountain. Towering, massive, awe-inspiring. It seems immovable.

Mountains in our lives, what are they? They are towering, massive, and seem immovable also. The mountains of sinful thoughts, grudges, overeating, selfishness, bitterness, and unbelief (you name them) have been there for a long time. We've gotten used to them. And we've gotten used to thinking that they can't be moved. What formidable fortresses!

A seed. A mustard seed. It is so small and looks very insignificant. Could any good thing ever come out of that? But wait, we can't see inside the seed. There is life hidden in that seed: a resting power, a tremendous force. That hidden power is from the Almighty.

And God says if we have faith as a grain of mustard seed, we shall be able to tell this mountain to remove hence, and it will. The seed of faith in God has boundless possibilities. The faith that takes God at His word and takes hold of His promises one by one is that which moves mountains. No, the mountains in our lives are not toppled in a day, but they are weakened and eroded as faith takes root. And to our wondering eyes, the day will come when we see the mountain disappear.

Praise God for what He has wrought in us by faith!

Praise God for what He will yet accomplish in us by faith!

Today

James 4:10-17

*M*end a quarrel,
Search out a forgotten friend.
Dismiss suspicion and replace it with trust.
Write a letter.
Share some treasure.
Give a soft answer.
Encourage a youth.
Manifest your loyalty in word or deed.

Keep a promise.
Find the time.
Forego a grudge.
Forgive an enemy.
Listen.
Apologize for a wrong.
Try to understand.
Reject envy.
Squelch gossip.
Examine your demands on others.
Think first of someone else.
Appreciate.
Be kind.

Be gentle.
Laugh a little more.
Deserve confidence.
Take up arms against malice.
Decry complacency.
Express your gratitude.
Gladden the heart of a child.
Take pleasure in the beauty
        and wonder of the earth.
Speak your love.
Speak it again
Speak it still again.
Speak it still once again.
Worship God.

Used by permission of "Keepers at Home."

To Forgive

Mark 11:22-26

*L*ife is a constant opportunity
    to forgive
        again and again.
I tell my children,
"One of the greatest lessons you will ever learn
    in life
        is to forgive."
Hurts,
    and wounds,
        and pain
            are a calling to forgive.
Every injury,
    every remembrance of an insult,
        is a calling to make a choice
            to forgive
                or not to forgive.
Every response
    to a wound,
        every reaction
            to a hurt,
        will have a consequence.
To choose not to forgive
    is choosing unforgiveness from God
        the Father.

To choose to forgive
is choosing forgiveness from God the Father.
To forgive
takes more,
much more,
than I have within me.
The flesh in me
rises up
to justify,
and retaliate,
and condemn,
and make judgments.
Then I cry out to my Father.
I remember the example of His Son
on the cross.
He endured and forgave
and did not retaliate.
I present to Him
my pile of ashes,
my neediness,
and ugliness
and ask for a measure of
power,
divine influence,
love and grace,
and mercy
to forgive
as He forgives,
so that I can be forgiven.

Forgetfulness

Psalm 103:1-5

*M*y forgetter is getting better. Sometimes when I'm at the refrigerator, I can't remember if I just put something in or if I were getting something out. It's good we don't have stairs. I don't have to wonder if I was going up, or if I just came down.

Preparing a fruit drink recently, I decided to add some home-canned pineapple juice I had noticed on my pantry shelf. At least I thought it was pineapple juice. I don't bother marking my jars, because I expect to remember what's in them. After adding the golden liquid to the orange and lemon juice in the pitcher, I eagerly tasted the drink. Ugh! It tasted strange and a little salty. I smelled the remaining contents of the jar. It was chicken broth!

Forgetfulness is good when I forget the things I ought to forget. Paul wrote, "Forgetting those things which are behind, and reaching forth unto those things which are before, I press toward the mark for the prize of the high calling of God in Christ Jesus" (Phil. 3:13, 14). I, too, want to forget past mistakes, sins that have been forgiven, and the memory of anything else that could hinder my spiritual progress.

On the other hand, the Bible instructs me not to forget the Lord (Deut. 6:12; 8:11, 14 and 19). I must not forget His benefits (Ps. 103:2). Besides, I must not forget to entertain strangers, do good, and share with others (Heb. 13:2, 16).

Lord, help me remember what I should not forget, and forget what I should not remember.

CHAPTER EIGHT

"My Grace
Is Sufficient for Thee"

2 Corinthians 12:9

When I Am Weak . . .

2 Corinthians 12:6-10

God keeps reminding me
    that in my weakness
      and in my neediness
   He's promised
     grace sufficient . . .
      perfected strength . . .
       the power of Christ in me.
Because of that grace (divine influence),
  He enables me
    to take pleasure in (to willingly accept)
     infirmities,
      reproaches,
       necessities,
        persecution,
         distresses
    for Christ's sake (not mine).
To take pleasure in
  adversity,
    frustrations,
     irritations,
      distresses
 is no easy thing.
   Self dies hard.
   I know that.
But I yield
  and willingly offer to Him

my weakness
and neediness
and remind Him
of what He promised me—

grace,
strength,
power,
to exchange weakness
for strength.

"For when I am weak, then am I strong."

When I Am Weak, Then Am I Strong

Daniel 3:13-18

*O*ur resources are limited. Our talents are imperfect. Our weaknesses are many. The circumstances are daunting. Feeling overwhelmed is common among mothers in today's world. What is a Christian response to overwhelming odds?

The Bible gives examples of Old Testament Saints "who through faith subdued kingdoms, wrought righteousness, obtained promises, stopped the mouths of lions, quenched the violence of fire, escaped the edge of the sword, *out of weakness were made strong*, waxed valiant in fight, turned to flight the armies of the aliens" (Hebrews 11:33, 34).

To be sure, they were not overcomers from the world's point of view. But in God's eyes, they were victors even though they suffered.

It is important we have the attitude of Daniel's three friends when they faced the smoking furnace. In short, their answer to this powerful king was, "OUR GOD IS ABLE to deliver us—we don't know if He will, but we will not bow to your idol!" This pattern of trust in a God who is able, no matter what the outcome, is the key to victory.

It is not the strong who are made strong, it is the weak. We must be committed to Him, and then our weaknesses can be turned into strength.

It's in His Hands

1 Peter 4:16-19

*I*n the past, I have struggled with difficult people, stressful situations, and problem areas in my own life. Then I came to understand Romans 8:28. God, in His infinite wisdom, allows nothing to happen to me that is not for my own good, because He loves me perfectly. Instead of trying to control and bear these burdens, I gave them to God.

To better understand this concept, picture God's hands cupped together, turned up, and ready to receive your burden or area of control. Place your burden into His hands and give this area to Him. This illustration has helped make the commitment more real to me.

Areas of control I have yielded to God are: my husband's schedule, our plans, church decisions, fears, and the future. Areas of perfectionism—perfect housekeeping, perfect children, perfect garden, etc., have also been committed to the Lord.

Dear friend, let me tell you how freeing this has been for me! Since God is in control and is taking care of my burden, I do not have to be in charge. My energies are now directed to serving Him, loving Him, and obeying Him. It's in His hands!

Child of My Love

Child of My Love, lean hard,
And let Me feel the pressure of thy care;
I know thy burden, child. I shaped it;

Poised it in Mine own hand; made no proportion
In its weight to thine unaided strength.
For even as I laid it on, I said
"I shall be near, and while she leans on Me,
This burden shall be Mine, not hers;
So shall I keep My child within the circling arms
Of Mine own love." Here lay it down, nor fear
To impose it on a shoulder which upholds
The government of worlds. Yet closer come;
Thou art not near enough. I would embrace thy care;
So I might feel My child reposing on my breast,
Thou lovedest Me! I knew it. Doubt not then;
But loving Me, lean hard.

                              –Anonymous

Trusting God's Viewpoint

Romans 8:26-31

*M*y God controls my life each day;
Whatever comes, whatever may
Appear as wrong
It passed His throne.
I walk a censored path today.

If Satan wants to ruin me
And make me falter angrily,
Can I by faith
Keep my soul safe?
With power from God walk cheerfully?

God's thoughts are higher, seeing more,
When He lets tests and trials sore
Cross o'er my way.
He wants to say,
"Grow strong in Me. My strength is more."
Oh, will a trial tear me down
And mar my features with a frown?
Or will a loss
Soon make me cross,
Before I view God's plan profound?

He gives me grace to help me through
Without the fret or feeling blue

That comes so quick
And wants to stick
If I don't trust God's point of view.

God's purpose is to make of me
A vessel that I can't yet see.
I trust His plans,
My faith expands
To rest and see His work in me.

My span of time and flesh will pass.
These sorrows, hurts, and wrongs won't last.
Eternal years
will hold no fears
For those who've stood the test and passed.

This is a challenge I try to live by. It can become a practice to ask, "What does God plan in this for me?" When David died so suddenly, this was my almost immediate response. With this attitude I can realize God's enabling grace.

Fear Not

Mark 4:36-41

*A*larmed to hear the chickens flying, flapping, and squawking, I rushed to the chicken house. What danger could be threatening our laying hens?

Somehow a tiny chick had found its way into the flock. As the curious chick moved about, the adult hens fled from it in terror. "Oh, you silly chickens!" I exclaimed. "Is that all it takes to frighten you?" Relieved to end their distress so easily, I caught the chick and put it outside.

I thought more about fear—in people. *Do I become fearful about equally small matters?* God has a completely different perspective than we do on the things that trouble us, and sometimes we fear when there is no need to.

Jesus' disciples feared death by drowning when a fierce storm tossed their boat. But the Master of the wind and the sea rode with them. Even in serious difficulty, He told them not to be afraid. Whether the problems facing us are large or small, Christ is near and reminds us, "Fear not."

Through the Valley

Psalm 23

*I*t was 9 o'clock and nearly time for bed when I called her. I had been praying for her when I thought of calling.

I knew Kristen, a single mother, would be putting her four children to bed too. Her three-year-old was on antibiotics because her ears were draining. I felt the go-to-bed time might loom like a mountain to her, depending on how the day had gone. And she might be getting up a few times in the night again too. I would just whisper into her home that I was remembering her as it came time to tuck all her children into bed.

When I phoned, her one-year-old and three-year-old were already sleeping. She was ready for a little chat.

Kristen did not fear mountains at bedtime. She eagerly shared some of the blessings of her day. A friend had faxed her some notes on Sunday's sermon from Psalm 23. The first phrase she commented on was, "Yea, though I walk through the valley." She pointed out that *through* implies there is a beginning and an end to the valley. That thought encouraged us both to hope. And also, we go *through* the valley, unless we choose to stay *in* the valley. (I enjoy her enthusiasm for God's Word.)

She continued, "Then there is the phrase about the shadow. We can remember the shadow is always bigger than the real thing, and that shadows exist only where there is light."

I knew she was reaching out to the light, not groping in

the shadow of the mountain that evening. I thanked God for her again as I retired. I had received a blessing at bedtime. I will walk *through* my "valley" also, guided by the Light ahead.

Rivers Among the Rocks

Job 28:9-11, 28

These are rocks—
jutting out
here
and there,
everywhere . . .
Big rocks.
Sharp rocks.
Jagged ones
and rough
on this pathway of life.
To scale,
to climb,
where to go
and how to go
I know not.
Neither do I understand
the why—
except that Father God
has ways
to humble me
to prove me
to know what is in my heart.

And in His time,
                not mine,
        "He cutteth out rivers
                        among the rocks."
And in those rivers
                I drink
                        deeply
                                and long
                                        and often,
                for in those rivers
                        are nourishment
                                and restoration
                                        and LIFE.

The Same Sun?

Deuteronomy 32:1-4

The blazing sun beat on the thatched-roof hut in Central America. Inside, a visitor told about the extreme cold he had left behind in Indiana. "The snow-drifts were so deep and the roads so icy yesterday that I could hardly drive to the airport."

A weathered native tilted her head, listening intently. "Sir," she asked finally, "do you have the same sun we do?"

Sometimes I almost ask the same questions, not just about the weather, but about God. When things go well, it's easy to think of God as good, kind, and loving. But when adversity strikes, He seems distant and cold. Is He the same God?

He is.

Job lost his riches, his ten children, and his health. Even then, he refused to curse God. "What?" he said to his wife, "Shall we receive good at the hand of God, and shall we not receive evil?"

Moses understood this idea, and he sang, "He is the Rock, his work is perfect: for all his ways are judgment: a God of truth and without iniquity, just and right is he" (Deuteronomy 32:4).

Sometimes "behind a frowning providence, He hides a smiling face." In stormy times or in fair weather, our God is good. Just as we have the same sun, we also have the same God.

The Storm

1 Peter 5:4-11

*W*hile preparing for my early morning walk, I discovered a white world outside. My heart sank. *Another* snowstorm! Two in as many weeks is unusual here. It would probably be another day without pay for my husband.

As I trudged along, I talked to the Lord about our troubles. Would the clouds ever lift? It had been tight for months. Our family had survived our first summer of market gardening. This winter my husband was picking up carpenter jobs here and there to keep us going until the next growing season. By now our finances were looking a bit grim.

I couldn't help noticing that, even though it was snowing and blowing, the robins were singing as cheerily as if the sun were shining on a spring morning. H-m-m-m.

Later as our family gathered in the living room for morning devotions, we noticed a small sparrow sitting on a nail under the porch roof. His feathers were all fluffed up, and he looked so serene, contented, relaxed—even cozy. He wasn't worried. Meanwhile, only a short distance away, the wind was still blowing and the snow was still flying.

Guilt came over me as I realized that, yes, I had been worrying. The tension eased as I remembered the words in Matthew, "and one of them [sparrows] shall not fall on the ground without your father." Of course! Jesus said we are of far more value than the sparrows. Surely God Himself put the tiny bird there to encourage me in my personal storm.

Willing for the Doing

Mark 14:38   John 4:32-36

*A*lberta bound! The decision to move had come after months of praying, asking advice, and deliberating. A small church had called, needing a minister. We were aware of the need and felt burdened for this struggling church. Yet our family had begun to feel settled again in Oregon since moving from Belize three years earlier. We thought of the children changing schools again, Delbert's carpenter work picking up steadily, the dreams we had for the old home place we were purchasing, and our love for the church where we were. It would have been easier to stay.

But the call had come, and we couldn't feel settled anymore. We did not want to move ahead without clear direction from the Lord. We laid it out before him and asked Him to reveal His will. He did. We were confident in His leading. Closing this chapter of our lives, we were ready to move on, trusting God for the unknown future. We were looking forward with excitement to what God would accomplish in that little church in Alberta.

Several months later I was tearfully talking to a sister about the difficulties of adjusting. I recounted how confident we were that the move was God's will for us. Now we felt uprooted. Little things like, "Where's that book, Mom?" or "I can't find the glue" irritated me. I explained how hard it is for the children—they look back to how wonderful it was in Oregon. The sister listened to my woes. I haven't forgotten her answer.

"Yes, we seek God's will for us, and we think we're ready

to do it. But living it out, and accepting what comes with it, is another story."

"Oh." That stopped me. I had expected things to go more smoothly. Yes, my spirit was willing, but my flesh was weak and wanted the easy way.

"Lord, make me willing for the doing."

Indian Village

Psalm 121

*O*h, God, I didn't ask to move back into this Indian village again. It was with relief that we left it 16 years ago."

But now we are here.

"For how long, Lord? How long must I endure these constant interruptions? The continuous flow of feet, large and small, at the door, asking, always asking to buy

eggs,
 beans,
  eggs,
   a needle,
    eggs,
     ice.

"Could I have a drink of water?"
"Do you have baby diapers?"
"I want to talk to your husband."

Then there is the din of the neighbor's drunken parties, (why did You put us by the town drunks?)

Babies cry. Always cry.

Oh, for the peaceful quiet we once enjoyed! And the refreshing hilltop view. Instead, I am shut up here next to a mountain that blots out most of the sky and stars.

"My child, this village needs to see Me. My witnesses in this dark place are so few. These children sent to buy need to feel my kindness, especially the persistent ones. Do the women know about the lasting friendship I offer? Let Me love them through you.

"The family next door needs to see *your* family living faithfully and happily by My commands, that there is more to life than wild carousing.

And then there are the passersby on the road:

on foot,

on bicycle,

or in jeeps.

You see them daily from your kitchen window. Pray.

"Remember, the cup of cold water given in My name has its reward.

"As for the quiet, have you failed to notice the soothing night song of the river? Babies are asleep then.

"Mountains are beautiful too. Pause often for the look into 'your' mountains' cool, green shadows. I Am there. I Am strength.

"And for how long? Leave that to Me. All I ask of you is faithfulness as My witness.

"Just for here . . .

now . . .

today."

"As thy days, so shall thy strength be" (Deut. 33:25b).

Trouble, Part 1

Psalm 71:1-12

*M*ommy, the bull is going to come in," worried two-year-old Melissa.

"He can't," I assured her, "the gate is shut." I calmly continued milking the cow while she eyed the bull outside the fenced enclosure.

A little later her distressed voice sounded close to me, "Mommy, the bull is going to come in."

"He can't come in, the gate is shut," I replied.

After this dialogue was repeated several times, I stopped milking. "Melissa, look at me," I prompted. With my arm around her, I spoke with firm assurance. "The bull cannot come in. The fence will keep him out." All fears allayed, she chatted happily while I finished my job.

My husband suffers from a degenerative nervous disorder. I worry. What if the disease claims his ability to drive? Or walk? Or feed himself? What if he becomes bedfast? What if I have to support a family of eight?

Like Melissa, I become more and more anxious, but God has fenced out future troubles. I can trust His fence to keep them out. What's more, if he ever opens the gate for those troubles to come into my life, they will still be under His control.

I find that worry peers through the fence at troubles; trust praises God for the fence.

Trouble, Part 2

Psalm 71:13-24

*L*ater on, the gate did open. Pushing his head through the crack, the Beast of Trouble forced the gate still further open. Then he thrust his feet and shoulders through.

Gradually my husband needed more help. First I shaved him and helped him bathe. Then I needed to write his sermon notes and letters and help him eat. At last he couldn't walk the short distance from the house to the truck without leaning heavily on my shoulder.

But Trouble was also a beast of blessing. He brought with him the quiet work of patience, the exercise of appreciation for David's wonderful sense of humor and other inner qualities and tender cords of love to bind us closer together. We came to experience the strength of calm trust in our heavenly Father.

Then, miraculously, Trouble retreated. Doctors changed the diagnosis and prescribed medication that greatly relieved David's symptoms. Once again his physical strength blesses our home.

Praise abounds for the retreat of Trouble.

But praise also rises for his entrance. For we discovered that God always stands between us and trouble and changes hurt to healing.

Nighttime—Tranquil or Traumatic?

Revelation 22:1-5

I used to like nighttime. When I was a teenager, I expressed my love for it in this poem:

> Nighttime is pleasant, sweet, and still,
> Beautiful, tranquil, and clear.
> Daytime is full of work and noise.
> To me the night is dear.
>
> Nighttime is silent, untroubled, calm,
> A time of peaceful rest.
> Daytime is filled with endless tasks.
> I do like night the best.
>
> Nighttime's when silver stars appear
> Like candles big and bright.
> Daytime finds the stars blown out;
> God saves them for the night.

My love for nighttime faded fast, though, when armed robbers started coming to our house several years ago. After numerous traumatic experiences, I hated to see it getting dark. I began to wonder, *Why did God make night?*

He gave me the answer through a song, reminding me that the night teaches me to trust Him, to put my hand in His. As I do that, my fear of night fades. Every night, whether tranquil or traumatic, is another opportunity to trust our faithful Father.

Why?

Isaiah 55:8-13

*T*he pats on the back and the words, "God knows best" helped very little.

"I know all the right words," I retorted. "I know what to say to others when it happens to them, but this time it's us. My brain *knows* all the Bible verses, but my heart doesn't understand."

When it happened, I cried, prayed, and pleaded. Vernon had accidentally dropped a hammer mill on the end of his finger and smashed it off. The doctor stitched the finger back together. For two weeks we waited with bated breath, knowing that if God willed, his finger would grow back whole. At first we were confident. After all, we had prayed. Many of our evangelical neighbors had interceded on Vernon's behalf.

Then we weren't sure. Although we could see live tissue behind the nail, the rest of the tip was black and hard. The doctor did not think it looked hopeful, but decided to try removing the dead material. If the bone were alive, he would do skin grafting to reconstruct the fingertip. I begged God to save it. Surely God would honor my request. Hadn't we gone through enough already? Didn't He know I was at the breaking point? He *promised* He would not send more than we *can* bear. Exhausted, I quit praying. I had cried myself out. I had given up Vernon to God.

I cannot say that "peace flooded over me" when I gave up my will to God, but I did feel better and was even able to face the idea of amputation.

As I was waiting outside the operating room, time dragged. What would be the outcome? Finally Dr. Caceres came out. Gently he told me he was sorry, but when he removed the stitches, the tip fell off in his hand. Some tears escaped, but I knew we had done our best. God had made the final decision. I had to accept that.

"In acceptance there is peace."

Crash

Romans 8:31-39

*M*y sister Judy had a life-changing car accident over four years ago. It was a severe jolt to have a zestful life thrown into reverse. Here was my world traveler sister waking up from a seven-week coma to discover she would have to learn to walk again. We marveled that she was alive and talking.

She did learn. It took hours, days, and months of hard work and therapists who believed she could. Judy has often testified how real God was, right there beside her, teaching her to walk again.

Then there was that right arm dangling disgustingly at her side. The hand that used to take prize-winning photos and create inspirational cards with them, now hung uselessly from a shoulder where nerves had been torn out by their roots. God's hand guided surgeons and therapists to work amazing (but slow) changes. With a few brilliantly simple adaptations around the house, Judy can manage by herself, and even takes photos with one hand—her left one.

More frustrating to my perfectly organized sister is a brain that now throws blanks in unpredictable places. Again, therapists have offered some help to compensate. Having to depend on drivers to take her places is especially exasperating for someone as independent as Judy used to be.

Face it. Life will never be the same. Professionals have done what they could. Friends continue to be extremely supportive. How can she lose faith in God, Judy says, when she depends so much on Him for such simple things as walking? Still, she has to face the tough questions for her own unique experience. What is God doing? Why? There remains the soul struggle to see by faith God's "bigger picture" in all this and to embrace it as her own.

The Hem of His Garment

Matthew 9:20-22; 14:34-46

I have had pain in my right side for over two years. Trips to the doctor became routine. First, the removal of my gallbladder seemed to be the answer. Then I had a litrotripsy to crush a kidney stone—but *still* the pain persisted. Whatever could be the matter?

I wearied of it all. I begged God to heal me. My heart cried out, "How can I touch the hem of His garment?" I wanted relief. It seemed I was always reaching, reaching . . . Where was God? Where was His healing?

After much soul-searching, I asked to be anointed. By this I acknowledged I had faith that God would heal me if he wished. I would accept His plan.

The service was simple. I had high hopes. I knew of miraculous healings. Surely God would heal me, for I, too, had reached out in faith and touched the hem of His garment.

Imagine my surprise when the pain grew worse. I tried to think positively. "Maybe it will get worse before it gets better. Perhaps the doctor can tell what the problem is now. It could be Satan is testing me." I leaned more on the Lord, asking His help to keep up my faith in Him.

The pain persists. I am thankful it is not as bad. The doctor feels adhesions may be the cause. I have faith God can heal me, but I also know His grace is sufficient for me. His strength is made perfect in weakness.

I am no longer reaching. I'm hanging on!

Purpose in Pain

Psalm 71:20-24

*P*ain has been my companion the last while. As I struggle to cope, I find that looking around me is far better than preoccupation with my own pain. Suddenly, I am finding many who are suffering more intensely than I am.

Does Jesus care about my pain? Jesus certainly felt compassion toward people He healed. Remember the leper who came to Him, begging to be healed. "And Jesus, moved with compassion, put forth his hand, and touched him, and saith unto him, I will; be thou clean" (Mark 1:41). Another example of Christ's compassion was when He healed the two blind men sitting by the wayside. Yes, Jesus cares about my pain.

Is there purpose in pain? I can choose to make this a "classroom" experience or a "prison" ordeal. Should I be earnestly praying for removal of this misery or for patient endurance? What is God teaching me? When I feel pain, I think of others suffering chronic pain. Day in and day out. No relief. But I see beautiful character coming forth in their lives—sweet, patient spirits resigned to the acceptance of God's will. Job, that patient man of God, illustrates this so beautifully.

When I feel pain, it deepens my trust in God. "Whom have I in heaven but thee? and there is none upon earth that I desire beside thee. My flesh and my heart faileth: but God is the strength of my heart, and my portion for ever" (Psalm 73:25, 26).

When I feel pain, I think of heaven. "And God shall wipe away all tears from their eyes; and there shall be no more death, neither sorrow, nor crying, neither shall there be any more pain: for the former things are passed away" (Revelation 21:4).

My friend, if you are in pain today, focus on what God is teaching you. The lessons will be invaluable. There is purpose in pain.

Dealing With Chronic Pain

Psalm 119:67, 71, 92, 107, 143

Physical pain is a personal suffering. No one else can know exactly how we feel. We are in it alone. When the pain becomes excruciating, we may find ourselves absorbed in a world of our own, unable to concentrate on anything beyond our pain.

When pain is a constant companion, we must learn to live with this unwelcome, uninvited guest! There are no easy answers to suffering but to accept it and try not to become absorbed with our bodies. God cares about our physical pain, but He is most concerned about the inner qualities He is developing in us!

Constant pain will rob us of our joy and enthusiasm for life if we allow it to. We need to focus on what we can do and not fret about what we can't. Following are a few tips for coping.

1. Learn to say no. You may want to give an explanation or just graciously say, "I am sorry."
2. Most people don't want to hear about our pains. Find someone you can share with, who genuinely cares. At times it helps to talk.
3. Do what you can. Don't use your illness as an excuse not to do the things you can do.
4. Try to be pleasant and cheerful, even when you are hurting. It doesn't matter to cry at times either.

Determine not to become grouchy and demanding. It is difficult enough for our families and those who love us to relate to our pain.

5. Rest when you need it. Don't overdo today; you'll pay for it tomorrow.

6. Find a hobby you enjoy.

7. Take time to enjoy nature: birds, flowers, and sunsets. Nature draws our minds toward God.

8. Read challenging books, biographies of men and women who have allowed God to work through their lives. Fill your mind with good thoughts. Meditate on God's Word.

9. Pray. When you are feeling too bad to read or pray, just rest in God's love.

10. Allow God to work in you, making you sensitive and caring to others who are hurting.

Great Physician, Do You Hear Me?

Luke 8:41, 42, 49-56

*T*uberculosis!

What a dreaded word! And our daughter tested positive, on the mission field and eight months pregnant with her first baby.

What can I do? I'm 3,000 miles away. Her doctor tells her to go home to have the baby so that treatment can be started immediately. But I call several physicians in the States who say she is better off in Belize where they are familiar with the disease. And there are varying opinions about treatment. One says she needs to be isolated from the baby once it arrives. Others say it doesn't matter. I spend hours on the phone with doctors and travel agents.

As I lay my weary, spinning head on my pillow, I think of the Great Physician. I cry out to Him to send healing, peace, and comfort in this difficult time.

Upon arising the next morning, I make a call to Belize. My daughter assures me that, although nothing has changed, the Lord has given her peace that He will be with her no matter what comes. Those words make it so much easier to endure the uncertainty.

The next few days, we rest in Him, confident that He is in control. The chest x-rays come back revealing that she doesn't even have the dreaded disease. The positive test meant only that she may have been exposed to tuberculosis.

We are thankful that the Great Physician is using her immune system to fight it off.

My health is in Your hand, Dear Lord,
  And the health of family and friend.
Often, Lord, You choose to heal,
  But sometimes You say, "Life shall end."
And when You choose to call us Home,
  Our voices in heaven we'll blend
In praise to You, who omnipotent reigns,
  And health or sickness doth send.

It Matters to Me
About You

Luke 12:4-7

*M*y child, I know thy sorrows,
Thine every grief I share;
I know how thou art tested,
and, what is more—I care.

Think not I am indifferent
To what affecteth thee;
Thy weal and woe are matters
Of deep concern for Me.

But, child, I have a purpose
In all that I allow;
I ask thee then to trust Me
Though all seems dark just now.

How often thou hast asked Me
To purge away thy dross!
But this refining process
Involves for thee—a cross.

There is no other pathway
If thou wouldst really be
Conformed unto the image
Of Him who died for thee.

Thou canst not be like Jesus
Till self is crucified;
And as a daily process
The cross must be applied.

Just as the skillful gardener
Applies the pruning knife,
E'en so, I, too, would sever
The worthless from thy life.

I have but one sole object—
That thou shouldst fruitful be!
And is it not thy longing
That I much fruit should see?

Then shrink not from the training
I needs must give to thee:
I know just how to make thee
What I would have thee be.

Remember that I love thee!
Think not I am unkind,
When trials come to prove thee,
And joy seems left behind.

'Tis but a little longer
Until I come again;
What now seems so mysterious
Will all be then made plain.

Take courage then and fear not!
Press forward to the prize,
A crown of life awaits thee,
Glory before thee lies!
                    —Alice C. Lefroy

Angels of the Lord

2 Kings 6:8-17

A few years ago I started to become unglued, and my poor nerves were ready to snap. I lived in fear. How very real and great was that fear! I was afraid to die.

I did not want to leave home. I just knew I'd be killed in an automobile crash. I did not even trust Vernon's driving. He took too many risks. I felt he didn't really care how afraid I was. I could imagine someone forcing us off the road, plunging us down a deep ravine. Those of you who have visited and seen driving in Central America can sympathize! Riding a bus was not thinkable. Whenever I traveled, I was on pins and needles.

I couldn't rest well at night. I feared going to sleep, afraid I wouldn't wake up. I was not concerned that I wouldn't go to heaven if I died, but I didn't want to leave the children motherless. How could they cope?

I was becoming a basket case. I told myself these fears were absolutely silly. I hesitated baring my heart to anyone about it—not even Vernon. I struggled alone. Praying didn't help. I faced a huge void. At last I could bottle it up no longer. "Are you afraid to die?" I blurted to Vernon one night.

He looked startled. "No. Why? Are you?"

Little by little, I poured out all my worries of the past few months. We talked, cried, and prayed. With victory came a great release. God is in control of my life. As long as I am following Him, I need not fear, for the angel of the Lord encampeth around me. He *is* taking care of me!

As Long as There Is a God in Heaven

Psalm 43

*D*epression with its mysterious darkness had settled down on me. Everything seemed hopeless. There was no way I could go on. I was a terrible failure as a mother. What made me think I could handle that role? And in our mission church, one after another had joined us only to pass out of the church again.

Failure haunted me, filling my weary mind with accusations. But worse than that, others wouldn't believe me when I said what a wretch I was. I had strong arguments, and I tried hard to explain to them "the way things are." They listened, and each one came back with hope for me. This only added to my list of failures. I had failed to get them to agree with me, as irrational as I was.

It must have been discouraging for those dear folks who listened, gave sound advice, and then heard me bluntly refuse it with, "That works for someone else, not me."

But gradually, the picture began changing. There was a little light at the end of the dark tunnel. I started listening to advice. The truth began to look like truth to me, and, bit by bit, I could believe what I was being told, that there was hope for me!

How glad I am today for God's children who stood on the solid foundation of God and His Word and offered that hope to me. I thank God for hope that came to me through prayers, cards, letters, words of encouragement and simple advice.

Dear Christian friend, don't ever give up on another person. Keep believing and offering hope. As one sister put it, "As long as there is a God in heaven, there is hope for you!"

Dealing With Depression

Psalm 142

*D*avid speaks about depression in the Book of Psalms. In Psalm 42:5, 11, he asks, "Why art thou cast down, O my soul." David was a man after God's own heart, yet he struggled with depression. This comforts those of us who also have had to deal with it.

We women are especially vulnerable because of hormone changes in our bodies, especially after pregnancy and during menopause. Of course, it can occur at other times as well. Depression is not sin, but we do need to deal with it.

Symptoms of depression:

1. An inability to sleep, a feeling of tiredness and lack of energy.
2. Crying for no reason, or uncontrolled crying when going through a difficult time.
3. A loss of appetite or overeating.
4. A deep feeling of sadness, anger, or despair.
5. Hopelessness, like a black cloud hanging over you.
6. Loneliness, as if no one understands or cares.
7. A loss of interest in things you usually enjoy.
8. Feeling worthless or guilty.
9. A problem concentrating, remembering, or making decisions.
10. Entertaining thoughts of suicide. (Get help immediately if you do.)

If you have more than five of these symptoms, you may be experiencing depression. We often hesitate to get help for depression, because it seems like a lack of faith. We do need to read our Bibles and pray. It's also important to confide in someone and ask that person to pray with us. There are times when we need to go to our family doctor and receive help with medication. It is not sin to use medication; feeling guilty will only make us feel worse. Obey the doctor's orders.

Help for the healing process:

1. Fill your mind with positive thoughts.
   Philippians 4:8

2. Recognize that the devil is out to discourage you.
   1 Peter 5:8

3. Forgive anyone who may have hurt you.
   Ephesians 4:32

4. Accept your physical weakness and limit your activities and commitments for a time (without feeling guilty).

5. Rest in God's love; He cares about you.

Rest and Be Thankful

Psalm 37:1-7

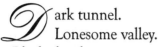ark tunnel.
Lonesome valley.
Black clouds.

These phrases describe my life just now . . . But what an opportunity to trust the Lord! In dark times like this it is easy to worry. Yet as a Christian I am not to yield to this temptation.

It is one thing to experience fear and quite another to have that fear running wild and out of control. The Bible talks about keeping our fears in check when it says, "and are not afraid with any amazement" (1 Peter 3:6b). We cannot have hysterical fear and be walking with the Lord the way He wants us to.

Fear, gloom, and self-pity are natural responses for me, but with God's help, I can live above these crippling sins. Although I am far from having arrived, here are some things that have helped me find peace in my circumstances:

1. Telling my heavenly Father, "I choose to trust You."
2. Prayer that releases troubling things to God.
3. Simply praying, "Lord, have mercy."
4. A mental list of tangible and intangible blessings I enjoy.

In conclusion, "be thankful and rest" is a thought that has lifted me many times.

Be Still

Psalm 46

I was in a valley so dark and, oh, so slippery under-foot. It was ominous and fraught with danger. I was anxious to go on, to get out of there and leave that awful valley forever behind. In my anxiety, I pushed forward on my own, groping for a passage through. All my efforts gained no relief. I only circled back to where I had started. What a disappointment!

I wept in that valley. I prayed faithless prayers. I panicked, bringing more strenuous effort, more endless circles, and still no way out.

Finally, I quieted my efforts and was still. I was ready for help, ready to listen. What wonderful relief that was! The valley was still dark, and I was in the same treacherous place, but there was blessed stillness in my soul!

Then I began to see that God was in that valley, too, and had been all along. In fact, He chose that valley to reveal Himself to me.

Step by small step, He began to lead me through. Often we delayed while I practiced being still before Him. As I learned to know Him and His ways, I gained confidence in Him. In quietness of spirit, even in surroundings that used to disturb me, I journeyed with God, my Guide, and my Stay.

Slowly we progressed, until one day I was in the light and turned to view the valley past. Great thankfulness welled up inside. When did we get through? I hardly knew. It was so long and painful, and so rich with blessings now.

I thank God for that valley now. No, I'd never ask for such as that! But He chose it for me, knowing just what would bring me to faith in Him. With Job, I could say, "I have heard of thee by the hearing of the ear, but now mine eye seeth thee." I had known many promises and could quote Scriptures, but didn't find them working in my life. When those precious words became part of my experience, my soul was thrilled! God's Word came alive, and praise God, I perceived Him as God!

"Be still . . .

and know . . .

that I am God!"

God Sees My Tears

Psalm 56:8-13

*G*od, You see my tears,
>   You know the deep pain,
>   the hurt, of seeing our child
reject You! Rejecting the things
>   we have taught,
>   and turning her back on all that is right.

God, You see my tears,
>   the deep pain, the suffering
>   from physical hurts.
The grief that comes from
>   sleepless nights filled with pain
>   when I feel rejected
>   by my own body.

God, You see my tears,
>   when a loved one has passed away.
>   Our loss is their gain.
We are glad for the glorious hope
>   of meeting again, someday in heaven.
But now, the parting, the separation
>   is so difficult.

God, You see my tears,
>   when I feel misunderstood
>   by those I love,
when there have been unkind words.

But, there is forgiveness and healing,
  and relationships restored
    because we love You, and care
      about each other.

God, You see my tears.
  Psalm 56:8 tells me
    that you put my tears into a bottle.
      They are written in a book.
And I believe someday
  that bottle of tears
    will be poured out as blessings
      on my head!

Jesus Can

Isaiah 61:1-4

Does your life
lie shattered
like broken glass
at your feet?
Let Jesus pick up
the pieces.
He can make a
WIND CHIME!

Are you
stretched
so taut
that you could snap?
Let Jesus pluck
your tightened
strings.
He can play a
MELODY!

Has life squeezed
and bruised
and crushed
your petals?
Let Jesus touch
your heart to
release His fragrance.

He can create
PERFUME!

Did the stream
of your life
hit a boulder?
Let Jesus shine
on the spray
of your
scattered
droplets.
He can paint a
RAINBOW!

Abused

Matthew 5:3-6

I was sexually abused when I was four years old. The memories were so terrifying and shameful that they were blocked from my mind until my life came unglued in a mid-life nervous breakdown. Then childhood scenes came back in vivid fragments.

Where should I begin for healing? I saw now why it was so hard to trust men and God. Trust was lost way back then. As I shared bits of my story with other women, they sadly confided, "Something similar happened to me."

I am not alone. There are many of us. Yet the horrible shame makes it a lonely experience. I didn't tell my parents until I was nearly 40 years old. No one wants to talk about it. Neither do I.

Now my spirit burns within me. I must tell of the path I found through rocks and storms to wholeness and peace. First, though memories are vague, I had to admit to myself that it happened. I couldn't deny or ignore it. It was there. I came to accept that it happened.

Then I learned to mourn, for they that mourn shall be comforted. It is easier to get angry at the outrageous violation. I was a human volcano when those long-buried feelings erupted, but it is sorrow that changes the heart. Sorrow for all I lost in childhood: trust, protection, safety, and more.

The next step is harder, and looks like a life-long process: to sorrow for my wrong responses to the abuse that have grieved the heart of God. This takes time, upheaval, and help from another child of God who has been through the school of suffering.

Meeting with the abuser to "close the account" (accompanied by two pastors and my husband) was so mechanical that I doubted we had gained anything until my next "emotional storm." Then I knew the stressful meeting had been worth it.

There is hope and there is healing.

Always Trust

Psalm 37:1-8

*L*ord, I don't understand You . . . I don't understand . . . At church tonight I heard Mark Carpenter was killed in an accident today. That leaves another family without a daddy. A 35-year-old wife. Six children ages 12 and under. A congregation without a minister. Lord, when You decide our times, why do you leave so many mothers to raise families without daddies?

Before I get too hard on You, Lord, remind me what helped pull me through those first years—those first days after David died.

The morning of David's death, he had led the family in prayer. "Lord, help us to *always* trust in You," he prayed in closing. Even in that moment, I reaffirmed my confidence in You as the Director of life's affairs for us, your children. David's life was gone three hours later, but we will *always*— we *want* to always—trust in You. It has taken an active practice of relaxing in You. I've found trusting You is more than believing in You, more than faith. Trusting is resting, not fretting. It's giving up asking "why" and knowing You have a right way for me to grow through *this* experience—*whatever* the experience.

I will pray for Karen and her young family. She's going to experience the empty chair, the quiet bed, the lack of advice, and the aching, bleeding heart. But may she *always* trust in You. This is my prayer.

Death—As I See It

Psalm 116

*O*ne gloomy fall day, the reality of death came to me as never before. An automobile accident snatched my dear daddy from this life. I didn't even have a chance to say "good-bye," or "I love you."

I walked around in shock those first few days. But I was thankful to God for sparing Mom, for kind friends, that Daddy hadn't suffered, and especially his testimony of love to God. As over 500 friends, neighbors, and relatives gathered to pay their last respects to Daddy, I had much to be thankful for.

But that was nearly two months ago. Today I miss Daddy—I miss him more than I ever imagined I would. I ache for Mom. I know she hurts, and I can't bear the pain for her. The tears keep coming and won't stop. Kind friends have forgotten and gone on with their lives while I'm still putting the shattered pieces together.

Dear God, I need You. You have promised to be a father to the fatherless and a comfort to the sorrowful. As I go through this painful time, show me what You want me to learn. Give me a glimpse of You, so I can sort through the duties which are so demanding—deciding whether they are eternal or only temporal.

Heal this hurting heart—in your own time. Give me the patience to endure the pain. Let it be a reminder to me of all the others who may be hurting and needing comfort.

Be with Mom, and show me when and how I can help her most, and when I need to stand back, and let You comfort her.

Thank You for giving me only one day, one moment at a time, and the strength to go through each one.

In Jesus' name I pray.

Amen.

CHAPTER NINE

"Continue in Prayer . . . With Thanksgiving"

Colossians 4:2

God Is Attentive to Our Prayers

Psalm 145:1-4, 14-21

Lord,

> There is so much to pray for;
> So many needs,
> So many people;
> And I hear you say, "Come.
> Bring your petitions.
> Bring your requests,
> Your children,
> Your congregation, your school,
> Your needs and desires.
> Lay them before Me.
> My ear is open.
> I will answer.
> I love to have you come."

> Lord . . .
> You have so many to listen to,
> So much to care for,
> Without hearing us each
>   individually.
> There are so many circumstances,
>   so many people . . .

and so many not prayed for,
that You are mindful of also.
I am astounded again today
that You remember me!
You are:

 a Fortress, in my storms of life,
 a Haven, when I am weary,
 a Husband, when I need counsel,
 a Father, when I am erring.

You are the Friend
 who listens to all I have to say,
You are the Answer for my heart cry.
Thank you for listening again today.
I needed this time
to think and meditate
 on You.

Prayer Partners

Colossians 4:2-6

*O*nce a month, my friend Marietta and I get together to pray. We have done it for the past four years. Having a prayer partner means so much. I often wonder how I survived before.

At each meeting, we share what has been happening in our lives. We jot things down as we talk. Marietta makes a list of my concerns; I make a list of hers. Then we pray. That's the best part.

Throughout the month, we pray for each other daily. At our next meeting, we tell each other about the amazing ways God answered our prayers.

Sometimes things come up between meetings, and I want and need prayer. Then I send a quick S.O.S. to Marietta, and ask her to pray for me.

The benefits of having a regular prayer partner are many. Sharing our burdens with each other makes them lighter and more bearable. When we pray, God's power is unleashed in our lives and in the lives of others. A valuable friendship deepens and a lasting bond forms.

I thank God for giving me a prayer partner.

Prayer, Communication With God

Malachi 3:1-6

Prayer is communication with God;
We pray and we expect
instant answers,
instant growth.
We forget that God's ways
are not our ways.
His answers may be different
than we planned.
He works in us
through hard and difficult experiences.
He uses the hammer, the chisel,
the refining fire, the fuller's soap,
to produce in us the answers
to our prayers.
We ask for patience;
instant patience, patience right now.
God brings people into our lives,
to teach us patience,
people who are not lovely,
who irritate us.

He brings disruption, changed plans,
 and we wonder, "Why, God?"
 And He answers,
"Patience comes through experience!"
We pray for compassion.
 And we experience pain,
  suffering, and grief.
  We cry out, "Why, God?
 How long must I bear this pain,
  this suffering, this grief?"
 He replies, "Tribulation enables you
  to bring comfort to others
  who need comfort, to be
  more sensitive to the pain, the
  grief of others,
  to become compassionate.
Prayer does not bring instant answers;
 but it develops spiritual growth,
  and maturity.
 Difficulties in life give us
  a longing for heaven.
 We learn to know God better,
  and we become more like
   Jesus!

I Was Going to Pray, #1

Nehemiah 2:1-5; 17, 18

I was going to pray ... first thing this morning.
    I was going to kneel and talk to God,
But the baby cried. Then I had to make breakfast
and pack the lunches, attach a button,
            and comb some hair.
In spite of the fact that it was time for school,
I made my tribe each
        sit on a chair, and I read the Word
            and prayed with them.
But it wasn't the prayer I had meant to pray ...
        a precious time of
        tender communion with the Lord.

I was going to pray ... but I quickly mixed buns,
    and a neighbor came to borrow some salt,
            and we chatted and talked
awhile of things that had nothing to do with salt,
    as we shared for a moment,
        a breath of eternity.

Then I bandaged a bruise, and my little ones
    came and begged for a story.
So I sat on a rocker, a child on each knee,
and smiled when they gawked at the story of Jonah ...
How the whale spat up and threw him out on the
    brine-washed rocks,

where he rubbed his eyes . . .
a startled, bedraggled, and wiser man.

And thus through the day I was going to pray.
I yearned for the peace I would find on my knees,
    alone in my closet of prayer.
            But instead I had to go and make peace
            and negotiate truces by sandboxes, toy bins, doll
            buggies, and swings. And once I went
            and did kneel down . . .
But the doorbell rang. It was someone asking
            for help. Just asking to use the tire pump . . .
            And how could I say, "I can't be bothered to
            fetch it, my friend, I was just going to pray!"

                                    –Margaret Penner Toews

Used by permission of the author.

I Was Going to Pray, #2

Hebrews 6: 7-12

*T*hen the children came home from school.
    Some piling on me their juvenile triumphs,
Some pouring their tribulations into my lap . . .
    (a mother's trophies).
I listened and learned. I eased a hurt.
I took one child too big for my lap, for a little while
    on my lap again,
    and told him we'd pray . . . and together
    we picked up his little problem
    and wrapped it up in a few small words
    and sent it to the heart of God.

Evening came, and I hadn't prayed. Oh, I'd talked in
snatches and interrupted sentences to my Lord . . .
but you know how it is with broken conversations . . .
    The threads get tangled.
Daddy came home and we had our supper.
Later, we gathered our little tribe. We read the Bible
    and prayed with them . . .
A circle around our family altar, childish babble
    silenced while Dad prayed to God.
    Then we tucked them in and kissed them all.
    The last demand for a hug . . . and water . . .
    had been allayed.

And finally, then, I went and prayed.
I knelt by my bed and laid my head on

the lap of God.
But I fell asleep. Then I dreamed a dream . . .
  I dreamed that He told me that through the day it had
  been His bruises I'd kissed away . . . that it was to Him
  I had told the tale of Jonah, hunched in the cavernous
  whale . . . that it was His problems I'd listened to . . . I'd
  loaned him the salt . . . and tied His shoe. He had
  come to my door to ask for aid . . . He got the buns and
  bread I'd made . . .

I woke with a start and went to bed
  And went asleep in the arms of God.

–Margaret Penner Toews

Used by permission of the author.

Suppertime Supplications

Ephesians 6:13-19

For the third time, our supper hour was interrupted, and for the third time a hush fell over the supper table. Another tardy young man thanked God for his food. I should have been glad he even *remembered* to pray; instead I was battling the same old frustration of a meal stretching out long and longer because of latecomers. I don't enjoy doing dishes at bedtime.

Suddenly I thought how I could redeem the situation. It surely came from God. *I* should also be praying during each pause. A good place to begin would be for the one who just arrived.

Thanks would be in order: for faithful VSers and a faithful son who all desire to live for God, and in so doing, lay down their lives for others. Thanks, too, for good working relationships with them, and that they patiently put up with *my* shortcomings.

Intercession: that God would keep them daily from evil; that they would be given patience for the frustrations of every day such as demanding people or uncooperative vehicles; wisdom and readiness to share on-the-spot devotions in church services.

It worked. My feelings improved.

Now I have another problem: their supper pauses aren't long enough!

Lift Them to the Lord

Psalm 61:1-4

*I*t happened again. We had to wait a half hour for the visiting family to bathe and get ready for service. True, they didn't know we would take them with us instead of having the usual afternoon service in their own village. However, the departure time for either service was the same. So they should have been ready.

My stormy thoughts raced as I considered their thoughtlessness. My turmoil continued as I tried vainly to concentrate on Brother José's devotional meditation.

Suddenly, I remembered something I used to do in these "helpless times" when people tried my patience and situations were beyond my control. Yes, how could I have forgotten? *Lift them to the Lord in prayer.* I chose to picture mentally the act of lifting that person up to the Lord in my arms. Then, having committed them to Him for His blessing and help, *I left them there.*

Tight stomach muscles relaxed (for emotions do affect our bodies), and I could rest in the peace of knowing they (and I) are in the hands of the Master Controller.

"And the peace of God, which passeth all understanding, shall keep your hearts and *minds* through Christ Jesus" (Philippians 4:7).

Prayer Reminders

2 Thessalonians 3:1-5

*D*uring an especially difficult and discouraging time, I wondered, Is anyone praying for us? Does anyone even remember we exist?

Just a few days later, we received a letter from a faithful friend in South Carolina. He wrote, "Our banana plants are finally doing well. I've committed myself to pray for your family when the banana plants remind me of you. I usually leave the pickup out by the shop. So in the mornings when going to work, I often pray for you because the banana plants remind me to pray for your family. Sometimes I wonder why dedicated people like your family would need prayers, but I know that's only a temptation from Satan to keep me from lifting you to God's throne of grace."

Tears stung my eyes. Our friend prayed for us. Regularly! He had chosen an effective prayer reminder by which he allowed God to remind him daily to intercede for us. Knowing this gave me fresh courage.

I started thinking about the prayer reminders other people use. I remembered a little handmade card a friend sent me. The children's home where she worked faced a crisis, so she made tiny cards requesting prayer for the institution. The card she sent me was only an inch square, but its picture of folded hands reminded me to pray.

A missionary in Nicaragua regularly sends out a prayer support letter. Whenever we get it, I read it aloud to the family at suppertime. We usually pray more for the work in Nicaragua right after getting a prayer support letter.

Years ago, a young man in Kansas offered to publish the prayer requests of the missionaries in El Salvador. *The Prayer Call* still goes out monthly to people committed to praying for our needs.

A missionary in Guatemala wrote, "I write the names of family, church family, missionaries, and other friends, far and near, on my clothespins. I'm reminded to pray for them as I hang up the wash."

What do clothespins, newsletters, and banana plants have in common? They can remind us to pray!

Comfort on Father's Day

Matthew 6:9-13

I recall the first Father's Day after David died. It started as a sad, dreary day. I didn't know how I could "move on" in it. As I sadly gathered the family to the table for breakfast, a thought came to me.

"We have no father," I said, "and no gift. But before we eat, let's each say something we like to remember about Daddy."

We started with Becky and moved on to Kimberly, each adding our thoughts. In that way we were able to reach into our hearts and "give him a gift." We were comforted.

I know our church family was praying for us and remembering our plight. We received several notes and a few scrapbook sheets that day to add to our book. We felt their support and a portion of comfort as they reached toward us.

But then to come home and sit at the table and be head of the family, with no David . . . I felt so weak. But as we bowed our heads to pray, another surprise came.

David had had a few memorized prayers we would sometimes pray together as a family. If he started the first two words in a slow deliberate way, we knew which prayer and would all join him in the prayer. As we bowed our heads that Father's Day meal, I started without having given it a thought, "Our—Father." The children all chimed in and we prayed, "*Our Father,* which art in heaven."

Yes, we have a FATHER. We are not left fatherless. In fact we have two fathers in heaven. Our Father, God, did not leave us comfortless. In that moment I felt His caring father-heart touch me, knowing He understands our needs. Every Father's Day since I have practiced using the Lord's Prayer as our noon prayer.

God, Do You Have Time to Listen to Me Today?

Psalm 73:23-28

*A*n unfamiliar pickup truck with an out-of-state license plate pulled into our driveway one morning. The breakfast dishes cluttered the table, and yesterday's folded laundry still sat on the loveseat. Toys and newspapers were scattered around the not-too-clean floor. I was just getting over the flu and had gone to bed the previous night, leaving the house in a very "lived in" shape.

While I started straightening things up, my husband went to the door. My thoughts were following the same pattern they always do when someone stops in unexpectedly and my house isn't ready for company. *Why don't people stop when the house is clean? Why don't they let us know when they're coming? We do have a phone!* But then the Spirit gently spoke to me and asked, "Do you have to make an appointment to visit with God?"

The brother who stopped wanted to ask my husband for some advice. As they shared together and sipped the tea I served them, I did the dishes. Meanwhile I thought about the many times I cry out to God in the middle of the day, or even in the middle of the night, and how He listens and meets my needs. I determined to be more willing for people to stop in anytime and to welcome them without partiality, regardless of my busy schedule or how my house appears. That day it happened to be a good friend with whom we feel a kindred spirit. But what if it had been someone with whom I felt uncomfortable or someone who stays and stays?

As I prepare for eternity, which is why I'm here, I want to remember that God and people are all who are eternal on this earth.

God Hears Women's Prayers

Psalm 4:3-8

*I*n a little bungalow in Belize, an elderly woman lived all alone except for rats that had invaded her home. They ate her food. They ran over her table. At night, they sometimes nibbled her toes.

In desperation, she prayed for deliverance from the pests. "Lord," she pleaded, "I don't know what to do about the rats. I leave it in your hands. Please do something."

Almost immediately, a cat arrived and moved in with her. She was a hungry cat, a good mouser. The rat problem disappeared!

God impressed on Nancy Stutzman the need to compile *More Tea Leaves.* Everything went well until her word processor gave out. One morning Nancy talked to the Lord about her dilemma. She reminded Him that she needed a typewriter or word processor or something. She left it in His hands to solve it however He chose.

Visitors came that day. They asked Nancy about her writing, and she told them her word processor had failed. They offered to take it to the States for repairs. Later, since it couldn't be fixed, they sent her a computer!

I hadn't seen Miss Kurtz, my favorite teacher, for forty-some years. When I learned that she would teach at the CLP Writers' Conference, I knelt beside my bed. "Lord," I prayed, "it would mean so much to me if You would let me be Miss Kurtz's student once more. Will You please let me attend the writers' conference?"

Not long after my prayer, I got a phone call from a friend saying that writer friends of mine wanted to pay my way to the writers' conference!

What happens when women pray? God hears and answers! Thank You, Lord.

Before They Call

Psalm 27:7-14

I focused my full attention on Laura's words.

"I tried some of Wilma's dresses, but they didn't fit. I went to Naomi's store to see if any of her ready-made ones would fit, but didn't have any success there either. I want to start wearing plain clothing, but I can hardly afford to buy all the material it would take."

Laura and her husband had recently accepted the Lord. They were regularly attending the local Mennonite church and wanted to join. She had been wearing a veiling for some time, but it looked out of place with the clothes she wore.

My mind went to my attic. There I had a stash of pre-marriage and pre-motherhood dresses in excellent shape. My body, unfortunately, no longer was. I had cherished a dream for too long, a dream of being able to wear those dresses again. Since the dream was no closer to reality than when I first dreamed it, I thought, "Why not give them to Laura?"

"I have some you could try, if you'd like," I offered. I was not sure they would fit, but at least she could try them on.

"May I, please?" was her eager response.

Later I went to the attic and selected seven dresses that had long lain dormant. Lovingly I packed them into a bag. As much as I hated to part with them, I wanted Laura to have them.

Later Laura phoned. "Kim, thank you for the dresses. They all fit as if they were made for me! Do you know what?" she continued, "When I thought about wearing cape dresses, I told the Lord I needed at least seven to get started. You'll never imagine my surprise when I pulled that exact amount from the bag! Sometimes I was uncertain; now I know God wants us to join the Mennonite church."

As I hung up the telephone, my mind went to Isaiah 65:24: "Before they call, I will answer."

Interceding in the Wee Hours

Luke 18:1-8

*W*hat was that noise? Our minds were too foggy with sleep to know where it came from. Nothing seemed unusual, but we were both trembling again. The weariness from loss of sleep and fighting fear after the break-ins was taking its toll on us. Again we knelt to pray, pleading the presence and power of Jesus and quoting Scripture for nearly one half hour till that horrible fear left and we felt the peace of God return to our hearts.

Many miles away, a mother, tired and weary, sat rocking her child. This was the second night she had lost too much sleep because her children had the flu. But tonight, instead of becoming frustrated, she felt God prompting her to pray—to pray for our family.

Later, she wrote us about this incident. After comparing dates, I realized she had been praying for us the night we battled the evil one.

Dear tired and weary mother... at 2:00 a.m. Maybe God woke you because someone needs your prayer intercession. Pray for whoever comes to your mind. You may never know till eternity what battle was won because you prayed instead of becoming frustrated. The devil may have triumphed that dark and lonely night had it not been for a dear sister praying while rocking her fussy baby.

Used by permission of Renita Gingerich.

Intercessory Blessings

Revelation 8:1-4

*M*issionaries, ministers' wives, mothers, and spiritual sisters all meet before the throne, lifting up the weak hands and faltering feet of a fellow sister. They bring her need before the Lord in prayer. The Spirit helps their infirmities, while angels present the offerings mingled with incense, which rise as a sweet odor before the Father.

These sisters, though separated by many earthly miles, bring this common request that unites them as one. They claim the promise, "If two of you shall agree on earth as touching any thing that they shall ask, it shall be done for them of my Father which is in heaven" (Matthew 18:19).

They pray. The Father hears and works.

The miracle of healing begins in their sister's life.

In Everything Give Thanks

1 Thessalonians 5:15-18

*M*y sister asked me to make a Thanksgiving banner for Sunday school. My pleasure!

I got down on my knees and spread the paper on our faithful, old hardwood floor. The cracks made good straight lines to keep my Old English script even.

At length, the black magic marker had squeaked out the last letter. I leaned back and viewed the finished product. "In everything give thanks."

But horrors! What was this? There on the floor was a faint shadow of the same message. The magic marker had leaked through the paper. Now what? "Give thanks," the floor winked back at me. But Mom had just finished having it sanded and had spent hours and days on her knees refinishing it to a perfect shine.

The stain was not in a corner. It was right in front of you as you stepped in the door. The funny thing was, I never heard one word of woe or scolding from my hard-working Mom. She took the message to heart and gave thanks. I was relieved of all bad consequences—and gave thanks.

Say, I think I'll just write that verse over all my mistakes after this—and my family's mistakes too. I'd hate to miss the blessings. I do want to cultivate and keep a thankful heart.

On Small Keepings

Matthew 10:29-31

One morning Daniel climbed an old windmill tower with a small battery and a cellular phone in tow. He wanted to see if the phone would work any better at that lofty height. Falling was a real danger, so he was extra careful. God kept him and he safely reached solid ground again.

That afternoon Daniel was helping a neighbor with the lowly task of "backing rice," carrying bags of rice on his back. He had stooped with his back to the pickup truck and hoisted one of the 100-pound bags onto his shoulders when his boot top caught on a bolt under the bumper, tripping him. He fell under the heavy weight, fracturing a bone in his leg. This time God allowed a calamity.

Thanks springs easily to our lips in the *tower* incidents, but how about the lowly and small goodnesses God performs for each of us countless times a day? That scorpion I *didn't* step on, the pitcher of milk that *didn't* fall off the table's edge, the dress seams that matched so perfectly I *didn't* have to rip and re-sew.

Recently I was making a dress. I had seen the spot of purple on the light green cloth and planned to arrange the pattern to avoid it. But I forgot about it. Later, cutting all completed, I discovered the purple spot at the very edge of a bodice piece. Though I had lost sight of the offending spot and forgotten to be careful, God hadn't.

Does God care for pitchers of milk and purple spots? I'm convinced He does!

Thank You, Lord, for keeping us in the "tower" events of

life, but a special thanks just now for the small things. Help me be more aware and more thankful.

I Don't Deserve This

James 1:16-20

I don't deserve this!"
This is how I am tempted to feel when some trouble or tragedy occurs. But when I stop and look at my blessings, I must also say in thankful awe, "I don't deserve this!"

I have a home, a comfortable home, and a happy family. I have children to love and enjoy. I have my husband's love and help. I don't deserve this.

I have a healthy body and can do my daily work. I have a sound mind. I thank God for these.

I have my needs supplied. We don't live in luxury, but I'm abundantly provided for. I have never been without a home or food or clothing. How blest I am!

I have learned to read. I have God's Word in my hands. Our home has good books, lots of them. I don't deserve these blessings.

I've had parents who loved me. I had a Christian father. He's in heaven now, and that urges me on in my Christian life. My dear mother is a constant source of blessing. I've had much godly influence throughout my life. I don't deserve such riches.

I have a church family, those who love the Lord and care for me and for each other. It's a loving brotherhood—what a place of refuge!

I have a dear Saviour who has washed my sins away in His own blood. I have the Holy Spirit as my comfort. I can call on my Father in heaven at any time.

The list of my undeserved blessings is infinite! May my

gratitude for all these blessings never lessen. Our generous God loves to bestow blessings.

O God, may I in return bless my fellowmen!

Propane Lights and Praise

1 John 1:4-10

The propane camper light does a wonderful job of lighting up our thatched roof kitchen. It hasn't always been so. Once, after a particularly hard wrench to remove the cracked globe from its makeshift wire holder, it fell to pieces in my hand. After that we had only the dim kerosene lamps for after-dark kitchen work. My gloomy thoughts matched the subdued lighting.

Imagine my delight when Daniel returned from town some days later with a new globe. Though it was smaller than the original, my husband's years of experience in making-do enabled him to come up with a workable solution.

Once again our kitchen is flooded with light, and supper dishes aren't quite the chore they had become. I can hardly get done expressing my pleasure over the improvement. My family never said so, but I wondered if they wearied of my repeated exclamations of delight?

Two spiritual lessons stand out clearly. One has to do with Jesus' LIGHT in my heart; the other, about my lack of praise over this glory. Too often my lips have been silent about His initial gift of salvation, as well as the daily keeping of my heart. Add to that the countless temporal and spiritual blessings He so generously showers upon me, His unworthy child.

Many times I have allowed the gloom of fear, doubt or discouragement to envelop my heart. Just as often, Jesus stands ready with the LIGHT of love, forgiveness, restoration and joy. He helps me trust and praise again.

"Oh, God, forgive my ungrateful spirit. You desire and are worthy of all the praise I can bring, and You never weary of it. Thank You for the beautiful, bright propane lights, but even more for Your glorious, darkness-dispelling LIGHT."

CHAPTER TEN

"I Will Open My Mouth
In a Parable"

Psalm 78:2

Washday Checklist

2 Corinthians 3:2-5; 4:1-7

*F*urlough travels took us to Michigan. It would be so good to see our friends again. We were unsure where they lived, so I began noticing the wash on people's clotheslines. "An Amish family must live there," I noted. A family's laundry tells a lot about them. (We did eventually locate our friends, but not by their laundry!)

Here in the village, wash hangs out any day of the week. Mine is in plain sight as well. Typical of any household, there is quite a variety. But untypical of some, grease spots still stain my men's clothes as they hang out to dry. Also, my lines hold many more towels and sheets than those of my neighbors.

Like it or not, the laundry of my life is on display too. What do those around me see? Do I show only the same commendable qualities as my non-Christian friends—hospitality that readily invites a caller in to find a seat and have a cup of coffee? Do I as freely share a baked goody as special to them as their "green corn" dishes are to us?

Are there "spots" of impatience, anger or hasty words many of my neighbors have? Am I free of gossip, refusing to pass on the latest village scandal?

Cleansing the "spots" leaves me ready to say, "I'm sorry," or "Forgive me" when I've been wrong. Consistency, honesty, and an abundance of Spirit fruit leaves a clean, fresh scent to honor my Lord.

Unlike my twice-weekly laundry days, my "heart-washings" had better be of the daily kind. I'm grateful God can give me a spotless heart, completely stain-free! And "hung out," it can be a testimony that honors Him.

My washday prayer: *Create in me a clean heart, O God, and renew a right spirit within me (Psalm 51:10).*

Worthwhile Fishing

Ecclesiastes 4:9-12; James 5:16

*A*lmost I carried my burden another day. I had already labored under its weight for a half a day and a night. This morning I hesitantly "unpacked" it before my husband; for I know the responsibility he carries for many other "burden bearers."

Daniel's solution was simple and easy. Why hadn't I thought of it myself?

Later, as I went about preparing breakfast, our smallest daughter sang in childish innocence, "Cast their nets on the other side, out on the deep blue sea." That message was meant just for me.

What had the night's fishing netted me? Nothing satisfactory. Only a whole draught of worries, gathering more of their own miserable kind.

On the *other* side, however, I netted relief and peace of heart.

Thank You, Lord, for a husband and a daughter whom You used to show me Your way.

Living or Dead Fruit Trees?

2 Corinthians 2:14-17

*O*n a visit to Honduras, we saw the effects of Hurricane Mitch. In one place, citrus trees stood knee-deep in soil the floods had washed in. They were all dead. But behind them stood other trees, healthy and flourishing. As we passed by, the lovely fragrance of orange blossoms wafted to us.

It was a picture of what was happening around us. Many Hondurans had lost homes, possessions, and even family members. Their hopes seemed dead. But from across the borders and beyond the floods, help arrived. Houses were being built; food, clothes, and medicines were being shared. Hopes revive as "trees" bear fruit and a sweet savor is going forth.

Another picture closer home, the church. Sometimes I am like those dead trees. Satan seems to come in like a flood, and around me so many sigh and cry with problems that I feel dead with discouragement too. But, there are still fruit-bearing ones *behind* me. Momentarily I forget they are there. A note of cheer, a prayer, or a small act of kindness gives me fresh courage to go on. Those dead trees in Honduras will never live again. Unlike them, I can again be a fruit-bearer.

What joy to be a part of the "living green," to be among those helping hands reaching out to others, to experience the satisfaction in united effort and a job well done. A sweet perfume is shed abroad to a watching, wondering world. What was said of the early Christians is still true today: "Behold, how they love each other!"

Dumb Chickens

Proverbs 25:23-28

I HATE this job. Why did I volunteer to feed these dumb chickens? Well, I love my husband, and he needed help today.

I loathe the way chickens gawk and crowd around me. Some squat in front of me as I try to walk. Their flightiness, curiosity and arrogance annoy me. Worst of all, some of them flee, then turn around and stage a frontal attack.

I waved the feed bucket at them. Suddenly, a statement I had heard somewhere barged into my mind. "The things that most bother you in others often reflect weaknesses in yourself."

"Oh, no," I argued. "I'm not like these chickens. Am I?"

I stepped over a hen crouched in my path. I thought to myself, "Doesn't she remind you of the way you freeze when a strange noise frightens you?"

I emptied the bucket and refilled it.

"As for curiosity, remember last week when a motorcycle ran into a ravine. Didn't you join the onlookers crowded at the edge to see the cyclist's corpse?"

A chicken, running away from me, suddenly turned and tried to peck my leg. ˙ kicked her aside, thinking, "At least I don't act like that."

"Oh, don't you?" my own thoughts accused. "Backbiting. Check the dictionary."

I emptied the rest of the feed, then hurried to the house. I had to know the meaning of *backbiting*. The Bible diction-ary gave this definition: "to speak evil of; this sin is warned against as being utterly unworthy of a believer."

The truth pecked at my heart. I couldn't deny it. I had recently talked about someone's faults. Now I hurried to wash myself and change my clothes. Free from the stench of chickens, I asked God to cleanse me on the inside too. I even thanked Him for what the chickens had taught me. Maybe they weren't so dumb after all.

My Horrible, Beautiful Finger

1 Corinthians 12:12-14, 26, 27

*R*ecently, I accidentally amputated the tip of my right middle finger. My husband rushed me to the hospital where a doctor reconnected the piece to my finger.

In the 12 days since, my hopes have gone up and down like a seesaw. On the third day, the doctor was cautiously optimistic. But on the fourth day, I smelled dead flesh. The doctor removed the sutures to discard the tip, but discovered that it had started growing together. He sent me home to wait longer.

Slowly sensation and warmth returned. *It's healing,* I thought. But the next day, my hopes fell. The tip looked like it was dying. One day it seemed firmly attached, the next day it felt loose again.

Preoccupation about my fingertip consumed me. I needed it. How would I type without it? I prayed for it many times a day. Carefully, I unwrapped the bandage again. Though the tip was dark and hard, I saw signs of restoration. I spent a lot of time looking at it. Other people almost gagged at the sight of it, but to me my finger looked beautiful. It was alive!

I understand better the verse that says if one member of the body suffers, all the members suffer with it. When my finger hurts, others of my members go into action to help it. My other hand bandages it. My feet take me to the car to go to the doctor. My nose sniffs for signs of infection.

The church is Christ's body, and I am one of the members. When another member hurts, do I care? Do I help? Am I as preoccupied about the welfare of the sisters of the church as I am about my horrible, beautiful finger?

Lord, help me care for my sisters when they hurt.

Pasture of Death

Ezekiel 34

*T*ires squealed, followed by a sickening thud, breaking the silence of the night. Eli and I ran out to the road. Neighbors joined us.

"What happened?" everyone asked.

As our eyes adjusted to the darkness, we saw it. A truck had hit a cow. Some neighbors flagged down oncoming traffic while others dragged the dead cow off the road. Still others tried to help the passengers of the damaged truck.

"Oh, she belongs to a man who lives several kilometers from here," someone explained. "He lets his cows roam along the road instead of renting pasture."

The excitement over, we all returned to our homes. We shook our heads as we talked about the irresponsible owner of the cow. This scene, with variations, happened within sight of our house seven times in the last five weeks. Four cows, a bull, a calf, and a horse were involved.

Though it is called the Pan American Highway, we have nicknamed the road by our house the "Pasture of Death." We wonder about owners who allow their animals to wander on a busy highway looking for food. What food can they find on a strip of asphalt?

In contrast, I think about my Good Shepherd. He doesn't turn me out to forage on a barren road. He leads me to green pastures of life! In addition, He stays with me and protects me all the time.

I am so glad that the Lord is my Shepherd.

Crazy-Patch Quilts

Ephesians 2:4-10

I love making crazy-patch quilts. In fact, right now I'd rather sew crazy patches than write for *More Tea Leaves!* I had to force myself away from the sewing machine because I knew I should be writing instead of crazy-patching.

I learned about this craft while on my way to my first CLP Writers' Conference. At a home where we stopped, a Mennonite woman was making a crazy-patch quilt. She sewed little pieces of cloth diagonally on a square fabric, and then joined the squares in a zigzag fashion. Her quilts, works of art, impressed me as a wonderful way to use up odds and ends of fabric.

Now I teach the method to Salvadoran women. They are delighted to learn how to use scraps and rags to make beautiful quilts. But, to my surprise, I am the one who can hardly stop sewing. Besides the satisfaction of utilizing things that seem almost worthless, I enjoy the challenge. I alternate bright colors and drab, dark shades and light hues. As the squares are sewed in place, I enjoy seeing the blends and contrasts of myriad colors.

I think about how God is working on the crazy patches of my life. The Master Designer plans the pattern of my life and sews it together. He alternates bright experiences with dark ones. When I think life is crazy, He is still in control. I am God's work of art. He knows what He's doing, and His pattern is just right. I delight in putting together crazy-patch quilts. Even more He delights in me.

That Terrible Dog!

Romans 14:10-13

*Y*ears ago, my ten-year-old son ran to me with tears streaming down his cheeks. Opening his hand, he showed me a shattered treasure—the broken pieces of his birthday watch.

"Look, Mama," he cried. "I found this in the yard. That Angie! Oh, that terrible dog! She ruined my watch." He glared at our Rottweiler.

"Where did you leave your watch?" I asked.

"I hung it on the clothesline to dry because it was wet."

"Son," I said, putting my arms around him, "I'm sorry this happened, but are you sure it was Angie? Your watch may have fallen off the line. The grass is freshly mowed. Can you guess what happened?"

He looked again at the pieces. They were chopped, not chewed. "The lawn mower went over it," he said sadly. "I thought it was Angie. Maybe she's not so awful after all."

I knew how he felt. Sometimes I make snap judgments. Too often I accuse someone of something they didn't do. Then I regret it. A lot of unhappiness can be caused with hasty conclusions.

No wonder Jesus said, "Judge not, that ye be not judged."

Am I hurting someone I love by my hasty presumption? I want to learn to be slow about concluding others have wronged me.

Lord, help me not to jump to conclusions, but to give the other person the benefit of the doubt.

Mixed With Faith

Hebrews 4:1, 2; 11:1-6

I use an old recipe for pancakes. The dry ingredients: flour, sugar, salt, and soda, are measured and stirred together. The vinegar and soda work to make light fluffy pancakes.

In our kitchens we often see what mixing ingredients will produce. The leavening agents yield no exciting results in their containers. Yes, the power and possibilities are there, but they are not active and working. When we mix them with the proper ingredients, behold the lovely cinnamon rolls, breads, pancakes, cakes, and a host of other goodies!

I find the phrase, "not being mixed with faith" an intriguing expression. When we know what God can do, but nothing is happening, maybe it's too much like the yeast, soda, and baking powder in the cupboard. Here in God's Word are His promises, purposes, and plans for us, but that Word with its powerful possibilities does not profit us until we mix it. Yes, mix it with faith, and watch the results!

Let Me Pout

Jonah 4:1-5

One day Tiana and I were in the van waiting for Vernon and Melisa. They were in the bank sorting through some mix-up. The wait seemed endless in the heat. Impatience began to rise. I wished I had a good book.

Tiana began whining. What could I do? I racked my brain for entertainment ideas. As I watched the people passing by on the sidewalk near us, I thought of something.

"Is that Daddy?" I asked when a crippled old man stumbled by. Tiana stopped complaining a moment to declare the man definitely was not her daddy. Soon she resumed her crying.

I scanned the sidewalk for more passers-by. I tried again with a fashionable woman with a painted face and high heels clacking noisily as she walked briskly on.

But my daughter would have nothing of it. She quit crying a bit to order, "Please be quiet, Mom; I'm crying!"

As she resumed her display of self-pity, I thought of the prophet Jonah, a notorious pouter. He sat on a hillside feeling sorry for himself because God took pity on the people of Nineveh when they repented. "How childish," we think.

What about us? Are there times when we wallow in self-pity, our minds centered on our miseries so that we cannot hear God speaking to us? Do we, in effect, tell the Lord, "Be quiet, I'm pouting!"?

What a Mess!

Genesis 6:1-8; 8:21, 22

*W*iping the paint from my brush, I stepped back, admiring my handiwork. The Rocky Mountains towered majestically in the background with tall pine trees in the foreground bordering a crystalline lake. It looked so serene.

I enjoyed working with oils. I felt a little like God must have when He created something and saw it was good.

Setting the painting back in my study to dry, I went about my normal duties. Later, I gazed with dismay at what had been my painting. Our 18-month-old "angel" had wanted to paint also.

Vernon was amused. "Looks as if we have a budding artist. Better take a picture of her 'first' painting." I wasn't in an appreciative mood.

My picture was ruined. A crumpled tube of blue paint lay nearby and my beautiful mountains were a disaster! The surrounding area of my study looked nearly as bad. How she managed not to get covered with the stuff herself was beyond me.

"What a waste," I thought. "It's good for nothing now."

Vernon was able to see something I hadn't noticed. "The paint is still wet. You can still salvage it."

It was worth a try. I went to work, wiping blobs of excess paint from the canvass, trying not to smear it any worse than Kendra Lily had. I was glad it hadn't been red or black paint. The blue had been the dominant color to begin with.

After the "renewal," I stood and analyzed it critically. It

was not quite the same as it had been, but still very lovely.

I thought how God must feel when we mess up His handiwork by taking our own way. How sad He must be when we go against His will, smearing our lives with sin. His blood can clean us up and make us beautiful again. I do not understand it, but I'm glad He can. What marvelous grace!

Whiskey Bottles

Ephesians 3:14-21

*H*ere in El Novillero we sell milk at the door. Folks bring all types of containers for their milk: Pepsi bottles, saucepans, pitchers, plastic bags, and many other kinds of containers.

It is the whiskey bottles I hate to see. I often wonder if the father of that child or husband of that wife used the bottle's contents himself, or did they get the bottle another way? They could have bought honey or something else in it.

Sometimes the labels are scraped off as if trying to hide the bottle's true identity. Others still proudly sport their brand names. Either way, it does not change the truth. It is a whiskey bottle. Always was; always will be. The bottle cannot help that it was made for whiskey. Though it can be used for milk, water, honey, or what have you, it is still a whiskey bottle.

God made individual people. It does not matter where we live. Living in Guatemala does not make me a Latin. I could adapt 100% to the culture here, but I would still be white. Always was; always will be. I cannot change that, but we can change what we contain. The Lord can empty us of the rotten stuff inside. Then He can fill our hearts with good: the milk and honey of God's Word, Christ's indwelling presence, and the power of the Spirit. We cannot change our "container," but, praise God, we can have a change of contents.

My Empty Pantry

Luke 11:5-13

*J*esus told the story of a person who went to his neighbor for bread because his pantry was empty, and a hungry traveler had arrived unexpected. This desperate man's request was honored in spite of its being late at night.

This illustration from our Saviour is a gentle reminder that we should not depend on ourselves to meet the needs of those who come to us. Fellow travelers on life's journey must be fed with bread from our heavenly Father's house. Our unexpected and needy visitors often arrive during times of personal darkness and need. There simply is no alternative to going to Him for bread. It is not pleasant to step out in the dark, even for friends. But the alternative is *no answers.*

Surely our Saviour would tell us an empty pantry is not a disaster, but rather, the real shame is our failure to approach Him.

Father, forgive me for the times I have proudly refused to disclose my own poverty. For the sake of those around me, I pledge to come to you.

Pruning for Production

John 15:1-8

*T*he velvety purple petunias were drooping in the midsummer heat. They were no longer covered with blossoms as they had been earlier in the summer. As I walked to the tool shed for the pruning shears, I meditated about the paradox of cutting back green foliage to stimulate flowering and more compact growth. How I hated to snip those deep purple flowers! Then I thought of how God, the Master Pruner, must prune those areas in my life that lack production.

What is it, Lord, that needs pruning in my life? Is it the way I lap up praise for my accomplishments? Help me to remember that my gifts and talents come from You, and not of myself. Praise for any accomplishment needs to be directed to You, the Giver.

Is it the way I serve the god of perfectionism in my life? Help me remember I cannot do anything perfectly, but I can be and am perfect in Christ.

Could it be those hidden motives of serving self? Help me to remember that nothing is hidden from You, O God. I realize the sinfulness of my flesh and want my life to be transparent.

My friend, what are the "petunias" in your life? The pruning process hurts, but the master Pruner is a careful gardener. He prunes with love and great skill.

Fill My Cup, Lord

Isaiah 12:1-6

The first years we lived in Belize, we owned a very old, undependable kerosene refrigerator. It seldom made any ice. At times the milk soured overnight. Roaches crawled through the cracks in the door. Yet, the refrigerator was a luxury, the only one in the village. Many times a day, people knocked at the door asking for "a cup of cold water."

I confess, sometimes the cup was given grudgingly. Sometimes I just filled it from the faucet, but a cup of water was given!

Many times I hold up my empty cup to God and cry out, "Fill my cup, Lord. I lift it up to You. I have become weary and tired and thirsty." God fills it up, not grudgingly, but freely. The cup is full and overflowing.

As I share that cup with others, God fills it, again and again. The thirsty soul is satisfied!

Let's Look Down Inside

Psalm 45:5-11

My child was grumpy
   Unhappy and sour;
   "A chip on the shoulder"
   It might be said.
   She seemed healthy.
   I checked on that.
   Not sick—then tired?
   Or done something wrong?
   I tried to encourage
   A look down inside
   To see what was troubling
   Or causing her mood.

   How often does God
   Take a look at me
   Saying, "What's the matter?
   Why so grumpy?
   Why so irritable,
   Downhearted, and blue?
   What is bothering you?"
   He tells me to take
   A look down inside,
   And He goes along
   To look through the gloom.

Together we look 'til we find the cause;
A selfish spirit,
A grudge I am nursing,
Trouble submitting
Lust for the forbidden,
Or disheartened with cares.

Together we look it over
And clean up the mess.
Then like my daughter,
Again I am free,
Happy and free.

Test Day

Psalm 119:33-40

*B*ecky sat up to the kitchen table with her Social Studies. Tomorrow is "test day." Tonight while she studies, she considers what tomorrow's questions might be. Now, she can find and learn the answers. She studies diligently in order to be ready for tomorrow.

God has given us an "open book" (the Bible) to study for "test day." I am beginning to understand how much He wants us to know the answers for the test. He wants us to know how to come to Him. He has the rules there which we must follow to pass the "finals." He gives us His Holy Spirit to abide with us, to open our minds and help us clearly understand the Scriptures. It thrills me that God on high has given us His Rule Book so that we can learn about Him and what He expects of us.

We find in 2 Timothy 3:16 and 17 that all Scripture is given by inspiration of God and is profitable for doctrine (teaching us), for reproof (showing what is wrong), for correction (to improve us), and for instruction in righteousness (training in right living) that we may be ready and equipped before God.

Papers and Pretties

Micah 6:3-8

I could hear the sounds of an unusual pre-breakfast flurry of activity in the kitchen. I smiled as I finished combing my hair. No doubt there was a birthday breakfast in the making.

I was surprised to find two of the children putting up blue, pink, and white paper chains. How pretty! Soon there was a disagreement about where they should be placed, so one ran off to help with the rustlings in her sister's bedroom. Frowning, she flounced back into the kitchen, "She is so bossy. She won't let me help wrap it."

I tried to soothe her as I continued breakfast preparations alone. She was still ruffled. "If you would just help me willingly with what needs to be done, that would be the best gift," I told her.

The shiny gift-wrapped parcel strategically placed by my breakfast bowl dimmed as I thought of the arguments.

Am I like that? Too often! Those special papers and pretties for God: organizing a ninetieth birthday party for Auntie Christina, sewing dresses for Brejida's three girls, or fixing an educational bulletin board for my homeschoolers are just that—pretties—if along the way I get impatient, proud, jealous, or angry. My special project "for God" takes precedence over doing His will.

How often does God tell me, "That's good, but really I am most delighted when you do My will. Speak kindly. Love freely. Praise me."

Trial

Luke 22:54; 63-71; 23:24

God, my son goes to court today—
on false charges.
How shall I pray?
My mother heart would like to pray,
"Let the verdict be, 'Not guilty,'
and deliver him from his enemy."

Your Son was in court too—
innocently.
The verdict was
"Guilty."
The punishment was
"Death."

I pray that my son, like Yours,
could accept the verdict of Your hand,
regardless of the punishment.
May he have compassion on his accuser,
remembering he is the ultimate loser,
not only in this case
but in life.
May he be able to pray
"Father, forgive him."
(But God, you know how glad I'll be
if the truth wins.)

CHAPTER ELEVEN

"Holding Forth the Word Of Life"

Philippians 2:16

Bible

Psalm 119:129-136

*T*his Book of Books alone will stand
    Forever and for aye.
This guide for youth and old alike
    Will light the darkest day.

Has any other book before
    Brought riches to the poor?
Or precious ointment to a soul,
    As salve is to a sore?

Brought peace to souls in throes of sin?
    Condemned the wicked's way?
'Tis comfort to a broken heart;
    A strength, a guide, a stay.

It changes hearts of clammy stone
    To hearts of yielding clay
Which God can fashion, mold, and bend,
    Committed to His way.
A constant Friend. No other book
    Has ever been so dear.
Earth's generations need this Plan,
    The same from year to year.

Not Guessing

John 14:1-6, 21-26

*M*ath was not his favorite subject, and those math facts (sigh)—there were so many to learn! Today the teacher gave him a page to do in 20 minutes. After laboring over the first few, he thought of a quick way to finish. He would just guess at the ones he didn't know. How pleased the teacher was that he had buckled down and finished in good time. Her pleasure was short-lived, however, when she began to check his work!

Why did he guess? He simply didn't know the answers and couldn't do his work. The teacher introduced number lines to help him understand. He was soon painstakingly correcting mistakes, but also gaining confidence. There *was* a way to find the right answer!

God, like the teacher, doesn't want us guessing our way through life or coming up with our own "easy" way, even when our answers seem ever so right to our human thinking. He wants us to come to Him and His Word for instruction. This is the right way to solve our problems and find direction for life. We can be confident we'll have the right answers and hear His "Well done!" in the end.

My Most Important Book

Psalm 119:10-16

*I*t wasn't there! "My blue notebook was in the side pocket. Right here. It's gone. And it is my most important book," I said in panic to the baggage man.

I had taken the short domestic flight to the international airport where I would fly to a Choice Books meeting. My lists, prayer requests, and phone numbers were in that book. Everything I needed was in that book. With it in hand, I felt "together." Without it I felt lost.

"Don't worry ma'am. If it is in the plane, we'll have it sent back here for you. You don't leave for three hours. We'll have it here."

I sat and waited. I prayed. I checked and rechecked. And prayed. At last I knew I had to go to the boarding gate. The baggage man assured me he'd still run it to me if it came on the next flight which was due to arrive in minutes.

It didn't come.

A message from God did. "Did you say *that* was your most important book? My Book was right beside it. I saw to it that you still have the Most Important Book. Trust Me with your lists and numbers. I'll help you remember what you need to remember. And only I can keep you 'together.'"

Lo-Cal

1 Peter 2:1-10

*M*y dad walked down the aisles of the grocery store filling his cart. Stopping in front of the salad dressing display, he looked at all the different flavors and types of dressings: Thousand Island, French, Ranch, Blue cheese, Italian—the selection seemed endless.

He picked up a bottle and peered at the label. "Lo-Cal," he read aloud. "Low taste," he muttered as he set it back on the shelf.

Nowadays, it seems, there is just such a variety in evangelical churches: Baptist, Methodist, Church of God, Brethren, and Mennonite. The list seems endless. People wonder why there are so many. There is a church to suit everyone's taste.

As a born-again believer, I must make a choice. Perhaps I was raised in a certain denomination. Maybe I feel the church of my fathers is right for me, or maybe I never attended a church before. In any case, I must choose one that teaches all the Bible. Watered down doctrine leaves a void. I must select one that is not low calorie. I must look for one that has the richness of God's Word, the flavor of Christian love, and the most essential ingredient of Jesus Christ as its base.

The Rule Book

1 Corinthians 11:1-9

A dear friend once showed me pictures of herself. In two of them, she had no prayer-headship covering. Disappointment stabbed through me. Not knowing what to say, I said nothing. I prayed for another opportunity to talk. I prayed God would guide my thoughts and words. Had she wanted me to bring it up when she showed me the pictures? This week I got to visit with her.

As I helped get dinner at her home, God gave me the words to open the subject. "I noticed on your pictures that you don't always wearing a covering.

Is 1 Corinthians 11 not important? Has God changed His mind, or don't you understand it?" I asked.

We faced each other frankly. "I am tussling with it," she replied. "I am not sure I have the conviction."

"Well," I said, "do you understand 1 Corinthians 11 to teach the headship covering and uncut hair for women taking their rightful place in God's order?"

"Yes, but I wasn't raised that way," was her answer.

"But God said it," I replied. "It is His rule. We must obey Him. I'm thankful He has given us rules for life. We can 'take it' and win, or 'leave it' and lose. His Word is what I build my conviction on."

She reached for my hand. "Thanks," she said. "It's a thing I tussle with. So many are taking it off. I knew you would feel this way."

I thank God He has given us a Book of instructions, so we can know His will.

Reflectors

1 Corinthians 11:10-16

*T*he little reflectors in the center of the road flashed by rhythmically. But something was wrong. Some of them were evidently crushed and unable to reflect brightly.

We were traveling home from a wedding in another community. I had been saddened by what I saw. Some of the young women were putting aside the headship veiling. Others were cutting their hair.

I understood their doubts. I had wondered too. If countless unveiled women are Spirit-filled believers, and walking with the Lord, why should I wear one? Is it necessary? Does this outward sign of submission to God's order have meaning?

The bright reflectors and the veiled women merged. Bright lights and veiled women show the way. Paths of submission to God's order are paths of peace and blessing, just as following bright reflectors help lead us safely. They are paths, examples to our daughters and others.

I thanked God for the privilege of wearing a veiling. He has certainly blessed my choice always to be veiled. My mere outward appearance draws attention to God and gains the attention of angels. Why should I choose less than the best?

I also prayed for those who had somehow been crushed by doubts or the opinions of man. I prayed they would reconsider and once more take their place obediently with the long line of faithful reflectors of God's glory.

Witnessing Through Your Walls

Ephesians 5:15-21

*T*he man was wandering alone
About the countryside one day.
Confused and troubled were his thoughts.
He needed help to find his way.

Unwatched, unseen, he neared your house.
And at that moment heard you say
A line of verse that gave him hope,
The shining words, "Take time to pray."

If he had passed while children quarreled,
Or heard a parent sharply say,
"Do stop, you children, straighten up!
Get back to work now right away!"
He might have said, "I don't think this
Would be a happy place to stay."

The things he hears will leave their mark,
To strengthen what you say,
Or tear away with ugly claws
The Christ-like life you would display.

Angry words, oh, let them never
From your lips unbridled pour.
At the moment that ye think not,
He may stand outside your door.

Jesus Is Lord

Psalm 34

*A*fter my father's tragic death in an automobile accident, my mother moved into a mobile home in our yard. Each year since she came, the yard around the trailer looks a little more like hers.

One day my brother brought an old sign that had been at the home place. It said "Jesus is Lord," with hers and Dad's names underneath it. He put it up, and below it parked an old wheelbarrow filled with impatiens. Everyone admired it. That is, everyone but me.

All I could think of was mowing around that wheelbarrow and two posts. They could at least have asked me, since I do the mowing. I decided to tell my siblings how I *felt*. Before I got it done, however, spring ran into summer; and now even summer was nearly gone.

One day, a car drove slowly into our driveway. A lady with two small children had a flat tire. She wondered if she could use the phone, but John quickly offered to change the tire for her instead. While the tire was being changed, she and I chatted. As she prepared to leave, she said, "I was scared to stop anywhere, but when I saw your sign, *Jesus is Lord*, I knew it would be safe to stop here."

As she drove away, I called, "Have a good day." But my mind was whirling. Suddenly, my gripe about the sign and wheelbarrow looked foolish. The blooms on the impatiens are a little brighter, and the old weather-beaten sign is still standing there, proclaiming to the world that *Jesus is Lord*.

Basics

Zechariah 4:1-10

Seeking souls that roam?
A word, a verse, a poem,
A love-filled home
Let Christ shine through.

Cheering hearts of gloom?
A card, a song, a bloom,
A sunshiny room
Show Christ is true.

It needn't be much:
A smile, a hug, a touch,
Heart things as such
Speak for Christ too.

Beautiful Toes

Psalm 18:31-36

*A*s a new missionary it was exciting to wash feet with a brown sister at my first Communion service overseas. When I stooped to splash water on her feet, I noticed her big toe stuck out and away from her other toes. *How strange,* I thought. And it wasn't very beautiful. I noticed other women's toes were the same. The older the women, the more likely the toes were deformed.

Then one day we asked a girl to guide us to a village buried deep in the jungle. She wore no boots, and her big toe gripped into the slimy mud as we labored uphill and down. Leaping from slippery tree root to mossy rock as gracefully as a gazelle, her great toe performed wonders. Now and again, she would turn and watch us with a bemused smile as we lumbered along, clomping, sloshing, and sliding in our boots. My legs were caked with mud past my knees. The back of my skirt was splashed brown to my waist.

As we broke into the clearing of the village, our guide stood in the first mud puddle, swished right foot over left, left over right, and just that simply, erased all signs of an hour's worth of mud. I needed the river to do a complete job.

The next time I bent to wash feet, I washed with great respect and admiration for that beautiful toe that stuck out.

Limiting God

Mark 8:34-38

I have never enjoyed sewing. I do it because I have to, not because I enjoy it. When we went to Belize as missionaries, I was very concerned that I would not need to be involved in any sewing classes. But, guess what? One of the first requests of the village ladies was, please teach us to sew.

God used that as one of the greatest blessings and opportunities of my life. Every Tuesday afternoon, ten to twenty women gathered at our house for sewing class. They learned to sew for themselves. We even sold some of the finished products, which allowed us to buy sewing machines and materials for our classes. But the greatest benefit was the opportunity to share a simple Gospel lesson and to win their confidence and friendship. God gave me the grace to do what I didn't want to do and turned it into one of the richest blessings of my life.

Does God ask us to do things we don't want to do, or don't enjoy doing? Would He ever ask us to go somewhere we didn't want to go? Do His plans always align with ours?

Many times we limit God. He delights in doing the impossible in and through us. When we submit to His plan and purpose for us, He always gives us the grace needed for the circumstances. God often brings rich fulfillment in the very responsibilities we thought we couldn't handle. Let's not limit God!

The Seed of a Saint

Luke 15:11-32

I saw him run headlong out of the bushes and across the highway. He hesitated by a tree in our front yard. I opened the door and asked if I could help him. He was shaking violently.

"Ma'am, this is sort of an emergency. Could you give me a ride to the crossroad?" This sounded like bygone days in Belize, not rural Ozark country.

We invited him in for supper, hot and ready on the table. Between spilling food and eating, he told us bits of his story. Someone was after him.

Though only 20, David's life had been shattered by tragedy. He knew little about the Bible and things of God. That evening we had the story of David and Goliath for family devotions. Our visitor had never heard it before.

After devotions, we took him to his friend's house at the crossroad. But at bedtime we heard a knock at the door. There was David again, eyes begging. "Could you give me a place for the night? My friend is scared of my pursuer too. I came back on foot through the fields."

In the black of night, a pony-tailed runaway asked us for a bed. What would you do?

Our Bible school teacher in Evangelism class told us to see the seed of a saint in every person we meet.

Seed has sprouted in unlikely looking places. Craig had had a long ponytail when he knocked on the door of a Christian home for help many years ago. Now he has been a missionary for years. Rene used to be a gang member.

Now he is administrator of a home for troubled men. Was this young, former gang member on our doorstep a future evangelist?

David stayed with us for several days. When he felt it was safe, we moved him to another community.

Has the seed sprouted? He is getting some Christian caring. Seeds have an opportunity to grow in that climate.

Los Angeles for Jesus

Isaiah 32:9-20

*L*ast summer Vernon, Susana, and I joined a street ministry team in Los Angeles. Although this type of mission work is very different from our work in Guatemala, we enjoyed it immensely. Every afternoon we spent a couple of hours on Broadway. There, teams of two took turns on nearby street corners passing out Gospel literature to the hundreds of passers-by. The rest of the group sang English and Spanish hymns.

Because we could speak Spanish, we did little singing, but spent the majority of our time offering tracts and cassette tapes. Most of the Hispanic folk accepted willingly, but the traffic lights and buses didn't wait for anyone. We missed more than we reached. How I longed to reach them all!

Leaving Broadway each day, we were saddened to see the sidewalks littered with our tracts! Apparently, a lot of people did not even bother to read them before pitching them aside.

Was the effort really worth our bother? Do people really want to know about Jesus? I wondered.

On Wednesday, we were at our motel eating supper when a Mennonite couple joined us. The wife's first words were "It's so great to see others that look like us." Later, they gave their testimony. They had been rock singers, searching for answers to life's problems. They had tried everything: counseling, medicine, the American dream, and different religions, but nothing helped. When their marriage failed, she became suicidal. Then two things happened that helped turned their lives around: Her boss gave her a tract, and on a trip east, the host of a Mennonite bed and breakfast had prayer with them.

These two small acts made such a deep impression on them that after Donna read the tract, she accepted the Lord. Her conversion was so dramatic that her husband soon followed suit.

Refreshed by this powerful testimony, we returned to Broadway with a greater zeal. Perhaps, just perhaps, one of these tracts would lead someone to Christ.

Elijah's Mantle

2 Kings 2:9-15

*I*t was September, 1981, the middle of the guerilla war. We two nurses and two teachers were the only white missionaries left in this part of Guatemala's steamy jungle. We had just received word on the radio that John had died. How he died wasn't mentioned, and it wasn't safe to ask over the radio. The voice over the radio said we were to come visit. It was a previously agreed upon signal that we were to evacuate the country immediately.

We began to pack in earnest. Some things stayed behind in a chest. The sugar, rice, and beans got divided out to church folks. Those things were given away as hasty farewell gifts, because our bulging baggage would contain no more. Could Don take it all in his little airplane?

Soon there were throngs of villagers at the door to see off the white ladies. Some came with tears of farewell, some looking for gifts.

Thud, thud, thud. Our luggage landed on the back of a villager's pick-up like clods of dirt on a coffin. It was so sudden. So final. We had no idea if we would ever return to the dear home from which we were being torn.

There was one more piece to load, the radio. Before we disconnected our contact with Guatemala City, we called to say we were going off the air, unless Mark at headquarters had a message for our young native pastor and deacon standing there beside us.

Mark, Raphael, and Catalino had worked together,

enthusiastically pastoring the small, but growing, flock in El Chal. Through the static crackling from the radio, Raphael and Catalino strained to hear Mark's message to be strong, of good courage, and faithful to their calling from God to church leadership.

It was as though the mantle of Elijah fell upon them. They squared their shoulders, flashed white smiles, and answered back. "By God's grace, we will."

What mantle did I leave behind?

Bloom Where You Are Planted

Philippians 4:8-13

I know a young missionary wife who complains chronically about her lot in life. To hear her, you might think she alone ever endured experiences such as she is facing. I get weary of her sighs. But I must not be too hard on her.

Lately I met another young woman who has been here for a few years. She startled me with a question. "How did you cope at first?" she asked. That brought back a lot of unpleasant memories.

I had coped as well as I could with the mentality I had. I had a "temporary" attitude. I felt life wasn't fair. I thought of my friends back home who did not have to worry about living far from nowhere with a howling baby, a toddler in the "terrible twos," no electricity, sometimes no water, and having their husbands off visiting most of the time. It wasn't fair!

Not only that, but I craved the "leeks and garlic" of the United States: Wheaties, Cheerios, Velveeta cheese, and other unavailable things. I could hardly wait until our term ended. Then we could go home and get on with our lives. I found life very frustrating.

We went home . . . and came back! After several years in Guatemala it finally felt like home to me. Then it dawned on me, that when I considered this my home, I was more content. I suddenly realized my "temporary" attitude had

gone, leaving happiness and peace. It's too bad I hadn't discovered that years ago.

A lot of people fall into this trap, especially missionaries.
Can we accept God's calling to be content where we are,
whether we stay the rest of our lives in one spot, or until He
leads elsewhere? We need to bloom where we are planted.

"In acceptance lieth peace." (Amy Carmichael)

The Lord Shall Preserve Thee!

Psalm 121

*Y*our furlough is over.
As you boarded the jet that would carry
You and your little family back to Belize
And responsibility,
I saw hesitancy in your eyes.

There will be no more
    Sleeping in, dishwashers, hot showers,
    Automatic washers and dryers.
    No more goodwill stores, Wal-Marts,
        and McDonalds,
    Coats and boots for the crisp, northern
        winter air,
    Grandpa and Grandma, aunts and uncles
        doting over Jerrel,
    Roast beef and mashed potatoes.

There will be
    Five-gallon buckets of water to be carried
    From the well across the street.
    The faithful old Maytag,
    Laundry drying in the tropical breeze,
    (And sometimes between showers,)

Little stores with the essentials,
Bare feet and sandals,
Rice and beans, the toot-toot of the
      tortilla truck,
Neighborhood chickens, pigs, and dogs
      in your yard,
And Spanish.

Along with these you will see
      Warm smiles from those who missed you,
      Visits from your seeking neighbors,
      Those who want to commit their hearts
            to the Lord,
      Victories in the lives of native Christians,
      Satisfaction when the day is done.

Some days you will
      Feel faint from the heat and heavy schedule,
      And long for the comforts of home.

But remember, dear,
      The comforts of home are temporal—
            they shall pass away.
      Support your husband in his work,
      Put your all into it!
      The seed must be sown, the truth shared.
      God will give the increase.
      They that sow in tears shall reap in joy.
            Psalm 126:5

Eternity is far too long
      To grumble and complain about the task
            He has given you.

Dear Daughter,

     Lift up your eyes unto the hills, from whence
          cometh your help.

     The Lord is thy keeper. The Lord shall
          preserve thy soul.

     The Lord shall preserve thy going out
          and thy coming in from this time forth,
          And even forevermore.

       (From Psalm 121)

CHAPTER TWELVE

"She Shall Rejoice In Time to Come"

Proverbs 31:25

The Empty Nest

Isaiah 43:18-21

*M*arriage began with the two of us
        deeply in love, happily anticipating,
           looking forward to a family,
                to children in our home.
The babies came,
    and we continued to anticipate,
        to look forward to
            the first tooth, crawling,
        then walking.
We couldn't wait till they could talk,
    till they were potty trained.
Then came the first day of school.
    Suddenly they became more independent
        and didn't need us as before.
Next came high school, driver's licenses,
    and we're saying,
        Time slow down.
           Where have the years gone?
Marriage, schooling, or job,
    and the nest is empty.
        Once more we are back
          to just the two of us!
There have been changes in our lives, our families.
    Our bodies are slowing down too.
        We're not as young as we used to be!

But, we discover, we are enjoying life.
There are grandchildren
to love and enjoy.
We're able to do some of the things
we always wanted to do.
God brings new challenges, ministries,
and opportunities into our lives.
We begin to anticipate and
look forward to tomorrow,
knowing that God is still using us.
He's not finished with us yet!

The Seasons of Life

Ecclesiastes 3:1-11

*W*hen I was young, I thought life crept slowly. Now that I have a 19-year-old daughter, I realize how quickly the stages of life pass. I remember when my mother took care of my grandmother, their roles reversed. Someday, I, too, expect to lovingly care for my mother. Life becomes a four-generation picture, each family member in a different season.

Spring is the season for new life, a time to be born. Flowers are budding, birds are nesting, and gardens are planted. We experience our baby's first smile, the cute expressions and questions our three-year-old asks in this season. As summer approaches, we realize how quickly springtime is passing. We struggle to hold each moment.

Summer is the season for preserving. We preserve godly principles and convictions in our children by nurturing with loving firmness. The tools we need for this season are praying hands and a pair of pruning shears.

Autumn is the season for letting go. As our children leave home, we fill the empty space in our hearts with memories of spring and summer. Our hearts are blessed to reap the harvest of godly children now establishing their homes.

Winter is the season for rest, for recollection. As we share memories with our grandchildren, godly values can be instilled from the wise lessons we have learned.

We pass through this life but once, my friend. Savor each moment, enjoy each season.

Unfinished Tasks

1 Corinthians 3:12-14; 15:58

*T*hose who know me know I am not a super woman. I tend to be a cluttered housekeeper. Although I love to have everything just so, I rarely do. I put a stack of papers into a box to be rearranged later at my leisure. There may be a coupon in the stack I definitely intend to use, or a letter I plan to answer quickly. But company's coming, and I must get rid of this mess! It usually turns out that when I finally get around to sorting the box of stuff, the letter is embarrassingly overdue and the coupon's expired. (Well, I just saved us some money by not buying that item!)

Now as I get older, I sometimes feel a little panicky. You see, I have a lot of dreams and goals in the box labeled, "To do before I die." The feeling of panic comes when yet another birthday arrives, and I realize I am no closer to accomplishing those goals. My life is probably half over, and there is still so much I want to do. One of those goals is to write a book. (*More Tea Leaves* has only whetted that desire.) My dream has been put aside for a more important one: to raise our children for the Lord. I've had to reevaluate my list of goals and eliminate those that no longer really matter to me. I had to decide which had priority. I needed to realize that I would not be able to do everything.

Although this bothers me some, I cannot help but think how much worse it would be if I were not completing the *most* important things in life. What about serving the Lord? Taking the time with *our* children when they are young?

Witnessing to that lady in the supermarket who asks why I wear the covering on my head? Or anything else the Lord may lay upon my heart?

I want to be faithful and do all He has asked, lest I should leave behind an unfinished task.

Showing My Age

Psalm 39:4-7

*W*ho is that old woman?" I sometimes ask myself when I see my reflection. I would still like to think of myself as a girl of 18. But the mirror shows me what I am—a woman growing older.

Many women fear aging; we shrink from it. Foolishly protesting, we try to hang onto natural beauty. Surely, a more important goal and more worthy of our efforts would be to develop inner beauty.

Time with God does that. When we read the Bible and allow it to work in our lives, and when we take time to pray, God's radiance shines in our personalities. We can be beautiful in the things we say and do. That kind of beauty never fades.

My mother is one of the most beautiful women I know. Her hair is white, her back stooped, and her wrinkles deep. Although she is ninety-two years old and has lost most of her hearing, she radiates joy and gratitude. She continues to serve God by sewing dresses for the needy. I want to be like her when I get old.

According to the mirror, I'm headed in that direction. I won't fear aging, however, if I remember I can daily obtain strength and beauty from God.

Ten Years—Many Changes

Hebrews 13: 5-8, 14, 15

en years ago, I was writing devotionals for *Tea Leaves*. Now I'm working on *More Tea Leaves*. Often I find myself comparing now with then.

We have endured difficult trials in the last ten years: Eli's kidnapping, unfaithful co-ministers and the resulting turmoil, and adjustments to changing responsibilities.

I have changed. Some of my dreams have faded. Weariness erodes my enthusiasm more often than it used to

Some projects into which I poured my energy are no longer mine. God has opened other doors of service and has given me much satisfaction as I accept new opportunities. Changes, while difficult, can be good.

Perhaps the greatest change is my relationship with my children. Ten years ago, our youngest was four. Now she is a teenager. Ten years ago, our children all lived at home. Now our two oldest sons are married, and we have six grandchildren. Ten years ago, I cared for my children. Now they are starting to care for me.

My husband's responsibilities are changing too. Eli is learning to be a follower, so that others can learn to lead.

So many changes aren't easy to make in ten short years. It comforts me to know we have an unchanging God. My circumstances vary, but He remains the same. When I go through painful experiences, He always cares for me. His love is constant. He is the same yesterday, today, and forever. I'm glad I can cling to His unchanging hand.

An Absolute Vision?

Psalm 126

*W*hy is life so complex? I look at a situation one way; my friend another. She thinks she's right; I know I am. Diverse voices vie for my attention and allegiance. I am weary of wondering who and what is right. In my heart I have a longing to rest.

Rest! I need to rest in Him knowing He has the answers to all the complexities facing today's church. I must rest, but not to the point I let go of the "line upon line, precept upon precept."

C.M. Battersby penned these words in one of my favorite hymns:

> If I have been perverse or hard or cold.
>
> If I have longed for shelter in the fold,
>
> When Thou hast given me some fort to hold,
>
> Dear Lord, forgive.

I must keep on! I cannot relax until He decides my time here is over. I greatly anticipate that glorious day! Time will vanish. Eternity will reveal the answers to many questions. Hearts will be united in the Land where we will all be able to see as God sees.

Lord, open my eyes to see my place in the spiritual conflict, in intercessory prayer and encouragement. And show me when I would do well to rest in You and wait.

> In Jesus' name,
> Amen.

Going to Heaven

John 14:1-6

I don't want to go to heaven. I want to go to Pennsylvania and El Salvador!" said our young daughter childishly. She wanted to visit favorite relatives. Why would anyone rather go to heaven? Her words shocked me until I realized she didn't really understand what she was saying.

As I thought about what she had said, it suddenly occurred to me that I may be guilty of the same foolishness. How often must my heavenly Father long to open my eyes to the bigger picture?

Our reasoning is also sometimes childish. Our actions prove that Heaven is not all that real or important to us. We want this or that or the other thing to happen in our way and in our timing. It is possible to become so involved in worldly pursuits and pleasure that we can forget who really is in control. We don't like interruptions to our plans! Our vision can be so shortsighted.

No one has seen the heavenly mansions Christ is preparing for those who love Him. Just like our children, we think we know what would be best for us. The Bible says God's thoughts are higher than our thoughts and His ways higher than our ways. Let's trust Him fully!

I Want to Go Home

Revelation 21:1-7

*B*rother Joe was preaching from his heart. He had flown from Romania, leaving his wife and family to brave it alone for a week. His stirring message was on the Macedonian Call.

"You know, sometimes it gets so hard on the mission field, I want to go home. I can hear it in the German I learned as a child. '*Ich vill heim gae.*'"

Suddenly my mind flashed back 11 years. The memory was as vivid as if it had been this morning. We had flown with our sick baby, Jonathan, from Guatemala City to Texas Children's Hospital for heart surgery. He died there. I wanted to go home. But we had no home or family in Texas. So we flew to Missouri for the funeral, within the comforting circle of my husband's family.

My heart was still not satisfied. I wanted to go home. We drove to Ontario to spend time with my family. Still, I wanted to go home.

What joy it was to journey back to Belize, to our beloved thatch roof house. It was dark and musty with jungle smells, but cleaned, oh, so lovingly by our dear mission family. Home at last! Home to waiting baby things . . . and no baby.

We sat down and cried in each other's arms. I heard my heart wailing louder than ever, "I want to go HOME!" Then I knew where Home was, and where I longed to be.

It is good our God touches our joy with pain, so that we yearn for better things than this world gives us.

Biographical Sketches

Each devotional is identified by the writer's teacup.

Barkman, Martha Stoltzfus (Mrs. Ervin), a native of Pennsylvania, taught school three years in the United States and two years in Belize, Central America. She and Ervin were married in 1981. In 1983 they were sent as missionaries to Belize and served in a remote jungle village, accessible only by travel across 50 miles of water or a day's walk. They returned to Lancaster, Pa. in 1987 and established a home business selling bread machines, grinders, wheat, and bread supplies. They are in the 12th year of homeschooling their 6 children: Clarita, Jana, Ervina, Claudia, James, and David. The family enjoys singing together. She says, "My favorite verse is Psalm 84:11. 'For the Lord God is a sun and shield: the Lord will give grace and glory; no good thing will he withhold from them that walk uprightly." I daily need the "sun" for light and direction, the shield for my protection, grace that is divine influence, and I don't mind being blessed with good things!

Birky, Joanna Hofer (Mrs. Delbert) was born in Alberta, Canada, and lived there until her marriage in 1977 to Delbert, a schoolteacher from Oregon. Delbert was ordained minister at Harrisburg, Oregon, a year after their marriage. The couple served at Maranatha Bible School and took care of foster children until 1982 when they moved to Dangriga, Belize, Central America, as missionaries. Childlessness, a difficult situation to accept, made them very grateful for the children God has given them through adoption: Joseph, James, Joyce, and Marvin. Early in 1993

Joanna was overcome by depression and later that year they moved back to Oregon. Joanna suffered much until the breakthrough came in 1996. The family is now living in Alberta, Canada where Delbert has charge of a church.

 Byler, Clara Gingerich (Mrs. Nolan) resides near Mt. Eaton, Ohio, where her husband is both minister and physician as well as chairman of Christian Aid Ministries and Deeper Life Ministries Board. Clara grew up in Kalona, Iowa, where she also taught school two years. That experience was a preparation for the past seven years of homeschooling. She is mother to four boys and four girls ranging in ages 19 years to two years. At this time she has five in school. For years her motto has been, "One day at a time." A verse she has come to love is, "For I know the plans I have for you, says the Lord, They are plans for good and not for evil, to give you a future and a hope."

 Glick, Mary June Lapp (Mrs. Melvin) is married to a pastor and lives in Dundee, New York. She grew up on a farm in Lancaster, Pennsylvania. Her husband was ordained to the ministry in Belize, Central America, where the couple served ten years. Myron and Michael were born in Pennsylvania before they went to Belize, and while there they adopted Melanie and Mauricio. The couple now has eight grandchildren and six foster grandchildren whom they enjoy entertaining in their cozy house in the woods surrounded by the beauties of God's creation. Mary June likes to accompany Mel in his mission and church responsibilities. Her favorite Bible verse is I Peter 5:10, "But the God of all grace, who hath called us unto his eternal glory by Christ Jesus, after that ye have suffered awhile, make you perfect, stablish, strengthen, settle you." Mary June lives with much physical pain and knows "perfection comes through suffering: not what we desire, but what God uses to make us more like Jesus!"

Glick, Verda J. Kauffman (Mrs. Eli), a former intensive care unit nurse and Christian day school teacher in Lancaster, Pa., is now a missionary in El Salvador since her marriage to Eli in 1966. Besides her duties as minister's wife (Eli was ordained in 1973) Verda has served as teacher of women's classes, Sunday School, and Bible School. She homeschooled their five children, Ernest, Philip, Timothy, Paul, and Karen. The three oldest are married and live in El Salvador. Ernest has been ordained bishop and Philip a minister. Verda recently closed her clinic that in 33 years served 33,000 Salvadorans. She now dedicates much of her time to writing and helping other writers. She keeps 16 writers' circles circulating, and her writing has appeared in more than 58 publications. Her book, *Deliver the Ransom Alone*, tells about Eli's kidnapping. Psalm 46:1 held special meaning for her the day her husband was held for ransom, as well as during the war and on many occasions when armed robbers frightened her and her family.

Martin, Susan Kim Glenn (Mrs. Vernon) was born and raised near Carbon Hill, Ohio. In 1977, she moved to Virginia where she taught school and worked for Christian Light Publications until 1980, then moved to Hagerstown, Md. She and Vernon were married in 1981. In 1982, Susana was born just prior to moving back to Va. In 1984, the Martins left the farm to serve in Palama, Guatemala, for three years. While there, Benji and Marvin were born. In 1987, they moved to Maryland but two years later, only two months after Kendra Lily was born, Kim, reluctantly, went back to Guatemala with her family, to serve under Mennonite Air Missions at El Novillero. Vernon was ordained to the ministry in 1994 and pastors two churches 10 miles apart. They have been there since Nov. 1989 where the youngest three daughters were born: Melisa in 1993, Tiana in 1995, and Lavina 1999. Kim is known as "the sweater lady" as she has a small knitting business to help provide jobs for Guatemalans. She also does some midwifery at times. Her favorite mottoes are: "Happiness is a flower; it grows where you plant it." and "Bloom where you are planted!" With all the moving she has done, she has learned it pays to be content wherever God wants her to be.

 Miller, Rebecca Anne Martin (Mrs. Verton) claims Ontario, Canada, as her homeland. Before marriage she worked as a rural clinic nurse in Guatemala until guerrilla warfare forced departure. She married Verton in 1985 and together they served in Belize, Central America, eight years. During that time they were blessed with four children: Jonathan, who only lived one month, Elizabeth June, and the twins, Jerald and James. After their move to Missouri, Caleb was born. In 1995 they moved to a new church outreach in Arkansas. There Anne suffered a nervous breakdown and has been healing ever since. She says, "Mothering a child with learning disabilities and taking time to relearn better thinking habits myself remind me to be patient. God has other servants to meet the world needs while He has called me aside for a season of personal pruning and growing. Writing More Tea Leaves has been a painfully effective tool to examine my heart, let God clean out hidden corners, and 'Renew a right (persevering) spirit within me' (Psalm 51:10)."

Moyer, Miriam Wenger (Mrs. David) moved with her family from Michigan to Kentucky in 1952 at age one year. There they began a mission church in the hill country in 1961. She and David (from North Carolina) were married in 1971, and the following two years David worked in a hospital in Georgia in alternative service. That completed, they returned to Kentucky, making it home for their eight children, Davetta, Evelyn, Dwight, Emily, Kevin, Delbert, Kimberly, and Becky. Evelyn passed away when she was nine years old, due to heart problems. In 1994, eleven years later, David died suddenly, leaving Miriam with six children at home and one married. Miriam's artistic abilities have helped her move into a home-based business of sign making. Her sons also assist her income by doing home repairs, a skill their father taught them. The book *The School of God* has made a deep impression on Miriam. When we see the Bible as our Textbook and God as Teacher, then all the happenings in our lives are lessons and tests to see if we are growing in godly traits. She says, "It has been a helpful perspective from which to view life."

Nisly, Brenda Stoltzfus (Mrs. Samuel) was born and brought up in Lancaster, Pennsylvania. While doing volunteer work at Hillcrest Home in Arkansas, she met Sam and they were married in 1978. The couple served in Hattieville, Belize, and Central America from 1983-1987, then moved to Partridge, Kansas. For the past nine years Brenda has homeschooled their 7 children, Rose Mary, Rhoda, Mark, Virgil, Verda, and Nathan. Even though there are times when she feels stretched to her limit, she wouldn't trade the opportunity. Three years ago they started a home business of market gardening and, more recently, baking. They find it a real blessing to have Sam at home and work with the family. She says, "The challenge is to be able to have right priorities in all the busy-ness and to trust God when finances are looking slim." A favorite verse which stems back to the morning of her and Sam's first date is Psalm 32:8. "I will instruct thee and teach thee in the way which thou shalt go: I will guide thee with mine eye."

 Stutzman, Judy Miller (Mrs. Daniel) married Daniel in her home state, Iowa, in 1976. God blessed them with six children: Julia, Anthony, Joyce, Janet, Jennifer, and one son who died soon after birth. In 1976 Daniel was ordained minister in Toledo District, Belize, Central America, and 13 years later he was ordained bishop. Consequently, Judy's life has centered around fulfilling responsibilities in their home and in the thirteen congregations for which Daniel is responsible. In their 20 years they have moved four times, and are now living in the village where they began. Village life is not Judy's choice, but she is content to rest in God's leading. A favorite verse is Psalm 68:28, "Strengthen, O God, that which thou hast wrought for us." She often prays this verse for herself, Daniel, her children, and others.

 Stutzman, Nancy Miller (Mrs. David) comes from Wellman, Iowa, where she married David in 1973. The following year they were sent as pioneer missionaries to southern Belize where they labored among the Indians. The couple has 8 children: Regina and Nathan (married), Konrad (died at age 6 in a tractor accident), Jonathan, LouAnn, Marsha, Melissa and Kenneth. From 1989 to 1992 they lived in Iowa where David was diagnosed with multiple sclerosis. His condition deteriorated in the next 5 years, resulting in Nancy caring for many of his personal needs. The diagnosis is now changed to Parkinson's disease and has been greatly relieved by medication. Nancy takes care of national and international communications for her fellow missionaries and homeschools her children. "One day at a time" has become Nancy's motto - a motto that counteracts worry and enables enjoyment of each "today."

 Weaver, Jo Ellen Scrivseth (Mrs. John) was born and grew up in northern Minnesota. In 1969 she married John. After living in Zanesville, Ohio, two years, they moved to Wisconsin where John was ordained to the ministry in 1976. The couple raised their five children on a dairy farm. Mark, Dan, Delvin, Kris, and Lovina are all married, and Jo Ellen and John have eight grandchildren. Jo Ellen says, "When our schedule becomes overwhelming with company, church work, and the temporal duties of life, I remind myself that 'People are more important than things.' By keeping this in mind I am given the wisdom to know which needs are immediate and the strength to do the task that is before me."

Christian Light Publications, Inc., is a nonprofit, conservative Mennonite publishing company providing Christ-centered, Biblical literature including books, Gospel tracts, Sunday school materials, summer Bible school materials, and a full curriculum for Christian day schools and homeschools.

For more information about the ministry of CLP or its publications, or for spiritual help, please contact us at:

Christian Light Publications, Inc.
P. O. Box 1212
Harrisonburg, VA 22803-1212

Telephone—540-434-0768
Fax—540-433-8896
E-mail—info@clp.org